Stress Control
For Peace of Mind

Stress Control
For Peace of Mind

Linda Wasmer Andrews

Main Street
A division of Sterling Publishing Co., Inc.
New York

This edition published by Barnes and Noble Inc.,
by arrangement with PRC Publishing

2005 Barnes and Noble Books

M 10 9 8 7 6 5 4 3 2

ISBN 0-7607-6468-9

For information about custom editions, special sales, premium and
corporate purchases, please contact Sterling Special Sales
Department at 800-805-5489 or specialsales@sterlingpub.com

Produced by PRC Publishing
The Chrysalis Building
Bramley Road, London W10 6SP
An imprint of **Chrysalis** Books Group plc

© 2005 PRC Publishing

The exercise programs described in this book are based on well-established
practices proven to be effective for over-all health and fitness, but they are
not a substitute for personalized advice from a qualified practitioner. Always
consult with a qualified health care professional in matters relating to your
health before beginning this or any exercise program. This is especially
important if you are pregnant or nursing, if you are elderly, or if you have
any chronic or recurring medical condition. As with any exercise program,
if at any point during your workout you begin to feel faint, dizzy, or have
physical discomfort, you should stop immediately and consult a physician.

The purpose of this book is to educate and is sold with the
understanding that the author and the publisher shall have neither liability
nor responsibility for any injury caused or alleged to be caused directly
or indirectly by the information contained in this book.

Printed in China

Contents

Introduction

Why Stress is Distressing

Reading a book about stress can be— well, stressful. It's true that stress can wreak havoc on both your body and your mind, contributing to everything from irritability, heartburn, and tension headaches to chronic depression, heart disease, and possibly even cancer. And it's equally true that some amount of stress is a virtually unavoidable part of modern life. Unless your name starts with Guru or your address is a remote tropical island, you're unlikely to ever lead a totally stress-free existence. So does that mean you're doomed to become yet another victim of stress? Not at all. While you can't eliminate all stress, you can get rid of some of it, and you can certainly learn to better control your physical, mental, and emotional response to the rest.

For some people, that thought alone is comfort enough. For others, however, it raises a whole new set of concerns. What if you try yoga and discover you don't like it? What if you have trouble finding a quiet place to meditate? What if you have good intentions about working less and relaxing more, but the demands of a hectic work or home life keep getting in the way? No problem! There are as many ways to reduce stress as there are to create it. If one method doesn't suit your personality or lifestyle, there's always another to try. If time is an issue, there are quick stress-busting techniques that can be wedged into even the busiest schedule. With a little patience and practice, you'll eventually find a stress management approach that works well for you.

Some of the techniques described in this book require 20 to 30 minutes, enough space to stretch out or move

around, minimal equipment, or a helpful partner. Others, however, can be done on your own, anywhere, anytime. The more effort you invest in reducing the stress in your life, the more benefit you're likely to see. But even small changes can add up to big differences in health and happiness over time. Baby steps will still get you to your destination, just less quickly.

Of course, some people are already quite good at keeping a lid on their stress level. Most of us struggle from time to time, however. Ask yourself if you ever feel:

- ❑ Irritable, anxious, or depressed?
- ❑ Tired all the time for no obvious reason?
- ❑ Burned-out in your job or life in general?
- ❑ Unable to sleep because of worries?
- ❑ Wound too tight or stretched too thin?

If you answered yes to any of these questions, chances are good that stress is at least partly to blame. At this point, you really have just two options: You can learn to control the stress, or it can continue to control you. Fortunately, picking the first option doesn't require spiritual perfection or a heroic level of dedication. It simply means learning how to relax and enjoy a calmer life.

Good stress, bad stress

Stress is everywhere in modern society. That's why, if you travel around Europe, you may overhear people complaining about le stress, lo stress, el stress, or der stress. In Japan, you may run into another term: *karoshi*, which means death by overwork. In the United States, a 2004 Gallup poll found that half of adults said they felt pressed for time, and three quarters said they were sometimes stressed out.

Surprisingly, though, stress isn't always a bad thing. In fact, without it, life would be mind-numbingly bland and boring. On the other hand, a little of the physical and mental arousal produced by stress can actually be motivating and energizing. Think about how you feel right before giving a speech. A slight case of nerves may provide just the energy boost you need to be extra sharp and alert. It's only when the nervousness spirals out of control that things begin falling apart. By that

Yerkes-Dodson Law

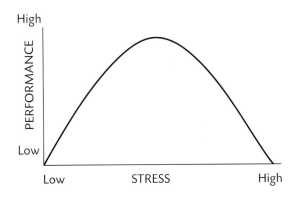

point, stress is no longer helping and has started hurting your performance.

Psychologists call this effect the Yerkes-Dodson Law. The law is named after Robert Yerkes and John Dodson, two psychologists who discovered a similar effect in lab mice almost a century ago. In humans, the law states that low stress often means low motivation and poor performance on a task. Performance and efficiency improve as stress and arousal increase—but only up to a point. After that point, performance falls off again as rampant stress begins to overpower everything else.

Hans Selye, MD, the Canadian scientist who was one of the founding fathers of stress research, recognized that stress had a good side as well as a bad one. He even coined the term "eustress" to describe helpful or pleasant stress, while he used the term "distress" for the harmful or unpleasant variety. Of course, when most of us talk about stress, we mean the negative kind, and that's how the word will be used throughout the rest of this book. But it's worth noting that stress can be a help as well as a hindrance, and the difference between the two responses is often just a matter of degree.

It's not necessary to eliminate stress altogether. Many times, all you need to do is dial it down enough to enjoy the arousing benefits without letting it get out of hand.

Fright, fight, and flight

What exactly is stress anyway? Actually, it's nothing more than your body's natural, protective response to a perceived threat. The threat sets off alarm bells inside your brain. The brain, in turn, prepares your body to fight or flee, which is why stress is also known as the fight-or-flight response. This rapid-response system is perfectly adapted to helping you survive a short-term, physical threat. For example, it will come in handy if you're ever confronted with a snarling tiger.

As your body goes into a state of high alert, your muscles tense in preparation for defending yourself or running away. Glucose, the blood sugar that serves as the main energy source for your body, comes pouring out from cellular storage sites into your bloodstream. Meanwhile, your heart rate, blood pressure, and breathing rate all increase in order to deliver glucose and oxygen to the muscles, where they're needed. Your mind is hyperalert, and your senses become sharper—the better to see and hear any hungry predator that may cross your path. At the same time, your immune system is temporarily revved up to prepare for possible injury or infection.

To conserve energy for fighting or fleeing, less urgent matters are put on the back burner. It doesn't make sense to waste energy on digestion, for instance, when you're trying to avoid winding up on the menu yourself. So while some physiological functions are increased, others—such as digestion, growth, and reproduction—are suppressed. In addition, pain perception is blunted, which will come in quite handy if you have the misfortune of being wounded.

It's easy to see how helpful these effects will be if you happen to run into a tiger the next time you go to the supermarket. Of course, it's much more likely that you'll run into long checkout lines, a maxed-out credit card, or a radio blaring news of the latest terrorist attack. Wrestling or running won't help you escape these kinds of psychological threats. Yet the stress response will still swing into action.

Unlike a wild animal that can be killed or evaded, the major threats we face today may last for weeks, months, or even years. Problems such as overcrowding, lack of job security, crime-infested neighborhoods, and marital conflict, for example, don't go away overnight. When stress is prolonged in this way, the strain of being on constant alert can take a harsh toll on your mind and body. This wear and tear explains how a protective response that is meant to help you survive can, over time, turn into an unhealthy reaction that leads to a host of mental and physical ailments.

Anatomy and physiology

To really understand the stress response, it helps to know a bit about the underlying anatomy and physiology. When you perceive a threat of any kind—real or imagined, physical or psychological—two different communication systems within the body are activated: the sympathetic-adrenal-medullary (SAM) pathway and the hypothalamic-pituitary-adrenal (HPA) pathway.

- **SAM pathway**—This pathway is the body's first line of defense in an emergency. It works through the sympathetic nervous system, the branch of the nervous system that initially mobilizes the body's energy and resources in response to a threat. The sympathetic nervous system triggers the release of two key hormones: norepinephrine (also known as noradrenaline) and epinephrine (also known as adrenaline).

- **Norepinephrine**—This substance is secreted by nerve endings of the sympathetic nervous system. It leads to a state of general arousal, increasing blood pressure, heart rate, and the level of glucose in the blood.

- **Epinephrine**—This substance has an even more potent effect on arousal levels than norepinephrine. Epinephrine is released by the adrenal medulla, the inner part of the adrenal glands, located above the kidneys. By activating receptors in the blood vessels and other body structures, it readies the heart and muscles for quick action. Epinephrine kicks the body's rapid-response system into high gear within a matter of seconds.

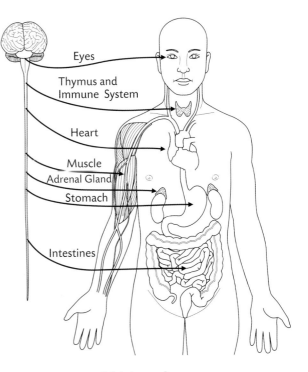

SAM pathway

- **HPA pathway**—This pathway originates in the hypothalamus, part of the brain that serves as the command center for the nervous and hormonal systems. When faced with a threat, the hypothalamus releases a substance called corticotropin-releasing factor (CRF). This substance travels to the pituitary gland, located at the base of the brain, where it triggers the release of adrenocorticotropic hormone (ACTH). Then ACTH travels through the bloodstream to the adrenal cortex, the outer part of the adrenal glands, where it stimulates the release of a powerful hormone called cortisol.

- **Cortisol**—This substance belongs to an important group of hormones, called glucocorticoids because they affect the metabolism of glucose. While epinephrine acts within seconds, the glucocorticoids exert their effects over a period of minutes or hours. At first, cortisol mobilizes glucose and delivers it to the muscles. Later, it promotes feeding and helps the body recover from stress.

A case of serendipity

We have Selye to thank for our modern concept of stress and its consequences. Back in the 1930s, Selye discovered just how harmful long-lasting stress can be. In later years, Selye became a celebrated scientist who was known for giving stress its name. At the time, though, he was still a young researcher making his share of blunders. In order to test the effects of a particular substance in rats, he needed to

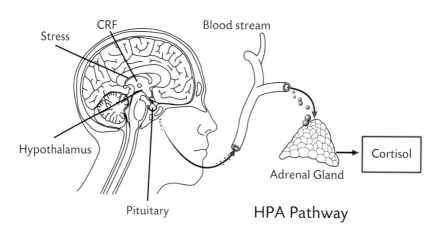

HPA Pathway

give the animals daily injections. There was just one problem: Selye was apparently rather clumsy. When he tried to inject the rats, he often wound up missing the mark, dropping the animals, and spending half the day chasing them around the lab.

After several months, it was finally time to examine the rats. Selye found that the rats that had received the experimental substance had developed peptic ulcers, enlarged adrenal glands, and shrunken immune tissues. At first, Selye was elated, thinking he had discovered the effects of the substance he was testing. His high hopes were soon dashed, however.

It turned out that a control group of rats, which had been injected with nothing but saline solution, had developed the same problems. When Selye thought about what the two groups had in common, he realized that all the rats had been subjected to the same inept handling, dropping, and chasing. It was the stress of this experience that had led to illness in both groups.

Of mice and men

They don't call modern life a rat race for nothing. Most of us have to cope with our own version of daily stress and strain. If the stress is prolonged over weeks, months, or even years, the accumulated strain on the body can lead to damage and disease:

- **Cardiovascular disease—** When people say that life is enough to give you a heart attack, they could be right. Studies have shown that long-term overexposure to stress hormones can lead to high blood pressure and atherosclerosis—narrowing of the arteries caused by a buildup of fatty deposits on the inner lining of the vessels. Chronic stress has also been linked to central obesity—excessive body fat in and around the abdomen. All of these conditions, in turn, increase the risk of having a heart attack or stroke.

- **Infections and immune disorders—** Stress has mixed effects on the immune system—the body's complex network of cells, tissues, and organs that protect against infections and other diseases. In the short run, it actually amps up the immune response. In time, however, the immune system may break down from excess wear and tear. Research has shown that people who are under stress have lowered resistance to the common cold. They may also have a decreased ability to ward off other infections. In addition, stress can lead to slower wound healing and poorer response to vaccines. When it comes to autoimmune diseases—conditions such as rheumatoid arthritis, lupus, and psoriasis, in which the immune system mistakenly attacks the body's own tissues and organs—stress sometimes seems to be a factor in flare-ups.

- **Cancer—** The immune system is also the body's defense against cancer, and there is preliminary evidence that stress might possibly play a role in the development of this disease. In addition, a growing number of studies have shown that lower stress levels can enhance the quality of life and potentially improve survival in people who already have cancer. However, there's no reason to believe that stress causes cancer by itself. At most, stress is probably one of several factors that together may contribute to the disease.

- **Other physical disorders—** Numerous other physical ailments have been linked to long-lasting stress as well. These include aches and pains related to muscle tension, such as tension headaches, backaches, and jaw pain. If you have asthma, stress can make your airways more reactive and lead to an attack. If you have a digestive disorder—such as heartburn, peptic ulcers, or irritable bowel syndrome—stress may make your symptoms worse. And the litany of stress-related complaints just keeps getting longer. Migraines, chest pain, infertility, loss of menstrual periods, insomnia, chronic fatigue, and lack of sexual desire are just some of the other conditions in which stress is thought to play a role.

- **Psychological disorders—** Unremitting stress can wear down your psyche, too. It's very common for people to respond to a stressful situation with irritability, nervousness, or a case of the blues. Over time, these emotional reactions may become habitual, developing into chronic hostility, anxiety, or depression. Untreated severe depression, in turn, may increase the risk of suicide—another possible

deadly consequence of stress. Eating disorders and substance abuse may also be triggered or worsened by stress reactions. Beyond that, there's even evidence that prolonged stress can destroy brain cells in the hippocampus, part of the brain that plays an important role in learning and memory. This may lead to an associated decrease in mental abilities.

It's the thought that counts

Stress is something that happens in your body. However, it originates in your mind. Earlier in the chapter, we defined stress as the body's natural response to a perceived threat. The most important word in this whole definition may be perceived. If you think of a situation as threatening—and especially if you view it as a threat with which you're ill prepared to cope—your brain will start the cascade of changes that make up the stress response. In short, you'll experience stress. On the other hand, if you think of the same situation as demanding but not threatening—and especially if you view it as a demand that you're well prepared to meet—you'll experience little or no stress. It's that simple, and that profound. Stress really is in the mind of the beholder.

So if stress is "all in your mind," isn't it possible to make it all go away through mental control? Theoretically speaking, maybe. Practically speaking, no. Let's face it: Some situations really are threatening, and it's doubtful that you'll ever train your mind to think otherwise. Even if you could do so, it wouldn't be a good idea. Remember that stress can actually be quite helpful when you need to face an enemy in battle or run for your life. In less life-threatening situations, a smaller dose of stress can give you the extra edge you need to be hyperalert and perform your best.

The problem occurs when the mind perceives a threat where there actually is none, the size of the response is out of proportion to the seriousness of the threat, or the response lasts long after the threat has passed. This is where mental control over stress really comes into play. By taking a realistic look at your situation, you can identify an exaggerated or overly persistent stress response. Then you can learn to turn it off or dial it down until your stress reaches a more appropriate level.

Fortunately, the body comes equipped not only with an on switch for stress, but also with an off switch. The body's natural counterbalancing mechanism is known as the relaxation response. In this state of deep rest, your heart rate decreases, your breathing slows, your muscles relax—in short, you undo all the physiological changes that were brought about by stress. The good news is that, while the stress response is involuntary, you can learn to call up the relaxation response at will.

Sometimes, often, always

As we've seen, stress is a reaction to something perceived as a threat. In psychologist-speak, the something that gives rise to stress is known as a stressor. Some stressors are very concrete: traffic jams, loud neighbors, a hostile boss, a vicious dog, or grief over loss of a loved one. Other stressors are more abstract: anxiety over your job, resentment toward a spouse, worries about the future, traumatic memories from the past.

Such abstract stressors are no less "real" in their effects than stressors that you can reach out and touch, however. Therefore, the key issue is not whether a stressor is physical or psychological. Instead, the critical factor seems to be how often stress occurs and how long it lasts. Based on these factors, psychologists have classified stress into three main types:

- **Acute stress—** This is the most common form of stress. It arises from current circumstances or ones that are anticipated in the near future. In small doses, it can be exciting and invigorating. In larger doses, though, it is simply overwhelming and exhausting. Overdosing on stress this way can lead to a host of short-term symptoms, including emotional distress, tension-related aches and pains, and an upset stomach. It's unpleasant but usually not harmful, so long as the stress doesn't become too frequent or long-lasting.

- **Episodic stress—** This type of stress involves frequent bouts of acute stress. People who suffer from episodic stress typically take on too many obligations, then find themselves torn between conflicting demands. Their lives may seem to veer from one crisis to the next. Some are classic Type A personalities, who tend to be hostile, competitive, impatient, and constantly rushing. Others are classic pessimists, who tend to be anxious or depressed, seem perpetually worried, and see the dark cloud behind every silver lining. Either way, they make themselves and those around them miserable. Yet the more they behave this way, the more it becomes ingrained and habitual. The physical and psychological complaints associated with acute stress may start to occur so often that they become chronic. Eventually, episodic stress can lead to the same kinds of serious health problems that are associated with chronic stress.

- **Chronic stress**—This type of never-ending stress saps all the joy out of life. It wears down the mind, body, and spirit with unrelenting pressures. It's the kind of stress experienced by people who feel trapped by a thankless job, an unhappy marriage, societal prejudice, or haunting memories from a past trauma. After a time, sufferers may become so used to feeling this way that it starts to seem normal. Yet, all the while, the constant stress is eating away at their health. If the downward spiral isn't halted, it can lead to a mental and physical breakdown. In the long run, chronic stress can kill through heart attacks, stroke, suicide, substance abuse, and possibly cancer.

If you suffer from acute stress, learning some stress control strategies can help you enjoy life more now, and it may help you prevent frequent or persistent problems with stress in the future. If you suffer from episodic or chronic stress, however, the odds are high that your mind and body are already paying the price. For you, stress control is a necessity rather than a luxury. The worse the problems, the more you stand to gain by learning some new stress management skills.

Living in the past

When you think of stress, you probably focus on upsetting events that are happening right now or that you worry may happen in the future. However, some events that happened in the past can also affect your stress level today. One striking example can be seen in people who experienced trauma or abuse as young children. On average, these survivors grow up into adults with depression and other stress-related disorders more often than people who had less distressing childhoods.

What's the link between then and now? On a psychological level, survivors of childhood trauma may develop a deeply pessimistic view of life, which increases their adult vulnerability to stress and depression. That's only half the story, however. On a physiological level, extreme stress in early childhood may actually alter brain pathways involved in the stress response. Specifically, recent research suggests that childhood trauma may lead to persistent overactivity by CRF, the brain chemical that sets much of the body's stress response in motion. This long-lasting, exquisitely sensitive reaction to stress may, in turn, predispose a person to stress-related problems later in life.

If you're a survivor of childhood trauma, all isn't lost. Your unhappy past certainly doesn't mean you can't be happy in the present. Nevertheless, it does mean you might have a heightened risk of depression and other stress-related problems—all the more reason to take preemptive action against stress now.

Yellow lights and red flags

Stress affects different people differently. However, these are some common warning signs of stress-related problems. Observe your own reactions for several days. Which of these signs do you show when you're under stress?

Physical signs

❑ Headaches

❑ Backaches

❑ Tight neck and shoulders

❑ Jaw pain

❑ Heartburn

❑ Stomachaches

❑ Loss of menstrual periods

❑ Lack of sexual desire

❑ Constant fatigue

❑ Frequent colds

Mental signs

❑ Difficulty concentrating

❑ Forgetfulness

❑ Pessimism

❑ Constant worrying

❑ Indecisiveness

Emotional signs

❑ Irritability

❑ Hostility

❑ Anger

❑ Depression

❑ Hopelessness

❑ Boredom

❑ Loneliness

❑ Anxiety

❑ Restlessness

❑ Panic attacks

Behavioral signs

- ❑ Substance abuse
- ❑ Chain smoking
- ❑ Eating too little or too much
- ❑ Sleeping too little or too much
- ❑ Impatient behavior
- ❑ Temper outbursts
- ❑ Crying
- ❑ Constant rushing
- ❑ Failure to get things done
- ❑ Frequent accidents

Social signs

- ❑ Social isolation
- ❑ Lack of intimacy
- ❑ Conflicts at home or work
- ❑ Loss of friends
- ❑ Intolerance toward others

Spiritual signs

- ❑ Apathy
- ❑ Joylessness
- ❑ Job burnout
- ❑ Feelings of emptiness
- ❑ Loss of direction in life

Other personal warning signs

- _____
- _____
- _____
- _____
- _____

Please note:

Many stress symptoms can also be caused partly or wholly by treatable medical conditions. If you develop new symptoms such as those described here, be sure to get a checkup by a physician to make sure they aren't due to a medical disorder. Also, see your physician or other appropriate healthcare professional if your symptoms are severe or if they last for more than a couple of weeks.

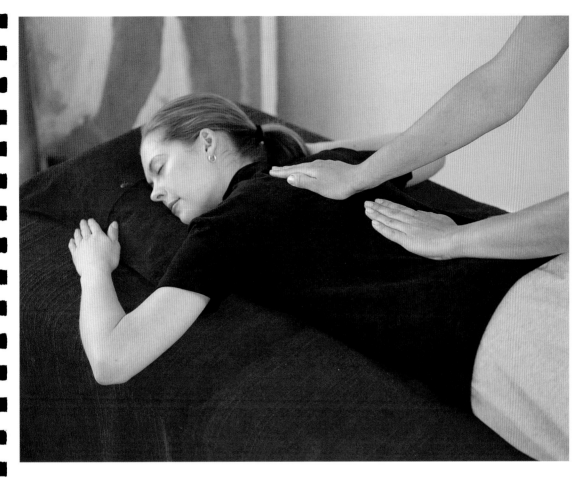

Take it or relieve it

If you checked just one or two symptoms, you may already be coping with stress relatively well, although there's always room for improvement. However, if you checked three or more symptoms, your stress level may be running amok. It probably is already affecting your quality of life, and it might be harming your health. You're overdue for learning some practical techniques to tame the tension.

It's all too easy to get caught up in a negative cycle, where stress causes symptoms, which create more stress, which makes the symptoms worse, and so on. This cycle can be difficult to interrupt—but not impossible. Pay close attention to how you're feeling, thinking, and behaving. When you first notice your personal warning signs starting up again, take prompt action. By using a stress control tactic at this early stage in the cycle, you can keep stress from getting out of hand.

Almost everyone—healthy or ill, young or old, male or female—can benefit from stressing less and relaxing more. This book will give you the tools you need to get started. In Chapters 2 and 3, you'll find an explanation of the relaxation response and the seven basic principles of stress management. In Chapters 4 through 10, you'll find descriptions of various stress management techniques. And in Chapter 11, you'll find several stress control exercises to help you put these techniques into action. Instead of fight or flight, you can learn how to breathe and relieve.

1: Self Test

How stressed are you?

This three-part self-test can help you gauge how stressed out you're feeling. It isn't intended to be a formal assessment, but it does offer a basic starting point for thinking about the nature and extent of the stress in your life.

Part 1

One of the simplest ways of rating stress is also one of the most useful. Simply rate how stressed out you're feeling on this scale.

1	2	3	4	5
blissfully stress-free	slightly stressed	moderately stressed	extremely stressed	breaking point

Ideally, you should repeat the rating once an hour for as long as you're awake. (But don't stress out if you miss an hour or two!)

Today's date: _____

Time	Stress Rating	Where You Were	What You Were Doing
1:00 a.m.			
2:00 a.m.			
3:00 a.m.			
4:00 a.m.			
5:00 a.m.			
6:00 a.m.			

Time	Stress Rating	Where You Were	What You Were Doing
7:00 a.m.			
8:00 a.m.			
9:00 a.m.			
10:00 a.m.			
11:00 a.m.			
Noon			
1:00 p.m.			
2:00 p.m.			
3:00 p.m.			
4:00 p.m.			
5:00 p.m.			
6:00 p.m.			
7:00 p.m.			
8:00 p.m.			
9:00 p.m.			
10:00 p.m.			
11:00 p.m.			
Midnight			

Rate your stress hourly for three or four days in a row. If you're employed, make sure that at least one of the days is a workday and one is a day off. At the end of the time period, look back over your rating charts to see if you notice any patterns. Are you a 1 or 2 at home, but a 4 or 5 at work? Does your stress consistently peak every day around dinnertime? Such patterns can help you target the times and places where using stress control techniques may help you the most.

Part 2

Life changes, whether major or minor, are frequently stressful. Most people realize that negative changes—such as a serious injury, the death of a loved one, or the loss of a job—can cause adjustment problems. But what you may not recognize is that positive changes—such as getting married, having a baby, or getting a promotion—can be quite stressful, too. Of course, no two people interpret the same event in exactly the same way. This questionnaire can help you assess how much change you've weathered lately and how much stress you've felt as a result.

For each event you've experienced in the past year, rate how much stress it caused from 1 (blissfully stress-free) to 5 (breaking point). If you experienced an event more than once, rate the most recent occurrence. If you didn't experience an event in the past year, give it a rating of 0.

Life Change	Stress Rating
Starting or graduating from school	
Filing bankruptcy	
Going to jail for more than 24 hours	
Changing to a new work shift	
Having a close friend die	
Having a close relative other than your spouse die	
Moving to a new home	
Getting married	
Getting divorced	
Having a son or daughter leave home	
Losing your job	
Separating from your spouse	
Making a major change in recreational activities	

Life Change	Stress Rating		
Becoming pregnant (or having your partner become pregnant)	■		■
Having your spouse die	■	■	
Changing to a new school		■	■
Taking out a mortgage or other large loan	■		■
Being the victim of a violent crime	■	■	
Getting together with family much more or less often than before		■	■
Developing new sexual problems	■		■
Being diagnosed with a life-threatening illness or injury	■	■	
Attending religious services much less than usual		■	■
Having many more arguments than before with your spouse or child	■		■
Being involved in a serious automobile (or other vehicle) accident	■	■	
Starting a new diet or exercise plan		■	■
Having much more or less money than before	■		■
Being promoted, demoted, or transferred at work		■	■
Reconciling with your spouse after a separation	■		■
Achieving something outstanding		■	■
Retiring from work	■		■
Taking out a medium-sized loan; for example, for a car or appliance		■	■
Losing your home or personal property to foreclosure or repossession	■		■

Life Change	Stress Rating		
Taking a big vacation		■	■
Being diagnosed with a serious, but not life-threatening, illness or injury	■		■
Having your spouse start or stop working outside the home		■	■
Giving birth (or having your partner give birth) or adopting a child	■		■
Building or making major renovations to a home		■	■
Having a new person move into your home	■		■
Making a major change in your social life		■	■
Changing your line of work	■		■
Experiencing a big change in conditions at work		■	■
Having a family member be diagnosed with a serious illness or injury	■		■
Totals from each column	Column 1	Column 2	Column 3

Add up your totals for each column. Based on the findings of researchers such as Thomas Holmes, MD, the life changes in Column 1 are events that most people find slightly stressful. The life changes in Column 2 are events that most people find moderately stressful, and those in Column 3 are events that most people find extremely stressful. Of course, you may have found a particular event especially easy or difficult to handle, based on your individual personality, circumstances, and stress coping skills.

Multiply your column totals as shown below. Add these numbers to get a grand total.

Column 1 Total: _____ x 2 = _____

Column 2 Total: _____ x 5 = _____

Column 3 Total: _____ x10 = _____

Grand Total: _____

Grand Total	Stress level due to life changes
0–19	Low
20–39	Moderate
40 and up	High

Many of the life changes listed on this questionnaire may be unavoidable. However, if such changes are creating a moderate to high level of stress, you need to make a conscious effort to relax and refresh yourself.

Part 3

Of course, not all stress is the result of major life changes. In fact, much of the stress in daily life comes from minor irritations and inconveniences that alone might seem trivial, but collectively can be quite aggravating. Your response to such everyday headaches and hassles can have a big impact on your overall stress level. This questionnaire can help you evaluate your personal coping style.

Indicate whether each statement below describes your thoughts, feelings, or behavior at some point during the previous week.

	Yes	No
1. I couldn't sleep because I had too much on my mind.		
2. I was always rushing, but still managed to be late.		
3. I believed things were never going to get better.		
4. I lost my temper and regretted it afterward.		
5. I felt anxious or nervous much of the time.		
6. I was impatient with other drivers on the road.		
7. I had a case of the blues and the blahs.		
8. I believed that I always had to win.		
9. I couldn't stop worrying about world events.		
10. I felt pulled in a thousand different directions.		
11. I believed that disaster was just around the corner.		
12. I was wound tighter than a spring.		
13. I blamed myself for something beyond my control.		
14. I felt guilty when I tried to relax and unwind.		
15. I thought of myself as a loser or a failure.		
16. I felt irritated when I had to wait in line.		

Count the number of "yes" answers you gave.

- Two or more "yes" answers on odd-numbered statements: You may have some pessimistic tendencies. The more affirmative answers you gave, the more deeply ingrained this attitude probably is. According to Martin Seligman, PhD, a psychologist at the University of Pennsylvania who is a leading authority on this style of thinking, pessimists tend to believe that bad events will last a long time and undermine everything they do. Such people also tend to blame themselves for whatever happens, whether or not it's really their fault. Pessimists not only see the glass as half-empty; they're also worried that it might contain toxic chemicals. Because they look for the worst in every situation, pessimists tend to create a lot of psychological stress for themselves. Mental approaches (see Chapter 5) to managing stress are often helpful for them.

- Two or more "yes" answers on even-numbered statements: You may have some Type A tendencies. The more affirmative answers you gave, the stronger these tendencies probably are. Back in the 1950s, cardiologists Meyer Friedman, MD, and Ray Rosenman, MD, first began to suspect that there could be a relationship between a certain cluster of personality traits and the risk of heart attack. They later dubbed this cluster of traits the Type A behavior pattern. According to Friedman and Rosenman, Type A people tend to be overly competitive, short-tempered, and impatient. They only have one speed: fast. Because such individuals are constantly hurried and harried, they experience lots of self-inflicted stress. Meditation and breathing techniques (see Chapter 4) can help them slow down without sacrificing their energy and vitality.

2: How to Stress Less

So much for problems. What you really need are solutions, and that's what the rest of this book is all about. As we've already seen, to reverse the physiological changes brought on by stress, you need to call up the body's relaxation response. While stress has been the subject of scientific research for a century, its opposite has only been studied scientifically since the late 1960s. That's when a cardiologist named Herbert Benson, MD, who was studying blood pressure in squirrel monkeys, was approached by several practitioners of a popular form of meditation. These individuals claimed that they could lower their blood pressure through meditation, and they wanted Benson to conduct research to validate their claims.

At first, Benson was reluctant, but the meditators were persistent, so he finally agreed to measure their physiological responses. He found that meditation did indeed lead to a decrease in their metabolism, heart rate, and breathing rate. In addition, it produced a distinctive pattern of brain waves, with fewer of the high-frequency waves that are typically seen during waking activity. Ironically, one thing that meditation didn't do in this group was lower their blood pressure. However, these individuals all had low blood pressure to begin with. Later research has shown that meditation can, in fact, lower blood pressure in some circumstances.

Benson dubbed this set of effects the relaxation response. It's a profound state of rest that serves as the body's natural mechanism for undoing the stress response. The great thing about the

relaxation response is that you can learn to turn it on voluntarily using nothing more than focused deep breathing. Meditation is another easy-to-learn method of calling up the relaxation response. If practiced regularly, the lingering effects can last throughout the day.

Relaxation

Relaxation alone usually won't cure what ails you if you're sick. However, when combined with standard medical treatments, relaxation techniques can help people with a wide range of mental and physical health problems feel better and enjoy life more. In scientific studies, the relaxation response has been shown to help people cope with the stress, pain, and other symptoms associated with a number of conditions, including:

- Anxiety disorders
- Depression
- High blood pressure
- Cancer
- AIDS
- Infertility
- Chronic pain

As you might expect, the effects of the relaxation response are the mirror image of those caused by stress. Heart rate, blood pressure, breathing rate, muscle tension, and metabolism all decrease. For this reason, the relaxation response can help counteract the harmful health consequences of too much stress.

Once you've learned to call up the relaxation response, you may notice a curious thing: You might feel not just back to your old self afterward, but actually better than before. Recently, Benson and others have begun to explore the biochemical changes that may underlie the relaxation response's positive afterglow. One theory, propounded by Benson, is that mentally letting go of a problem may trigger the internal release of nitric oxide (NO), a gas that is the molecule du jour in many research labs today.

As NO permeates the brain and body, levels of the stress hormone norepinephrine may spike briefly. After that, however, the NO counteracts the norepinephrine and other stress hormones, causing the brain to release certain neurotransmitters, which function as chemical messengers. These neurotransmitters include dopamine and endorphins, both of which are linked to feelings of pleasure and well-being.

Equal and opposite reaction

The stress response activates a branch of the nervous system known as the sympathetic nervous system. In contrast, the relaxation response activates the parasympathetic nervous system, an opposing branch. Instead of fight or flight, this branch helps you rest and digest. It promotes relaxation and conserves the body's energy and resources. The parasympathetic nervous system is the system that is working overtime when you're lying on the couch, lazy and drowsy, after wolfing down a big meal.

Time for a little R & R

Calling up the relaxation response isn't difficult. Two basic steps are all it takes. One is focusing on a repeated word, phrase, sound, or activity. The other is passively disregarding other thoughts that may come to mind. When your mind starts to wander, there's no need to wrestle it into submission. Instead, all you need to do is gently guide your thoughts back to the repeated focus point.

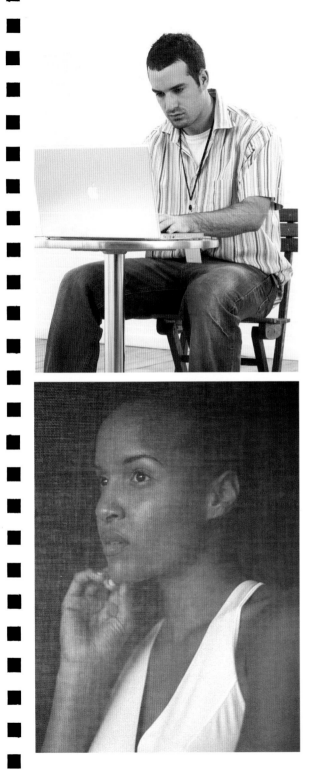

These are some general guidelines:

- **Time—** For many people, the best time of day to call up the relaxation response is first thing in the morning, because this gets the day off to a calm, positive start. If your family tends to have hectic mornings as everyone rushes off to work and school, it might be worth setting the alarm a bit earlier to give yourself a chance to relax first. But if the very thought of doing this makes you want to bury your head under a pillow, pick another time—maybe during your lunch break, your child's naptime, or right before dinner. If you have trouble sleeping, try practicing the relaxation response at bedtime.

- **Place—** Ideally, you should find a quiet place where you won't be disturbed. This doesn't have to be an isolated mountaintop, however. If you're at work, close your office door, and have an assistant or voice mail pick up your calls. If you're at home, close your bedroom door, and ask your spouse to watch the kids for a few minutes. If you enjoy the outdoors, try your backyard or a pleasant location in the local park or botanical garden. The key is to find a spot that feels safe and doesn't have too many distractions.

- **Position—** Any comfortable position will work, whether sitting, lying, kneeling, or standing. Many people like to sit in a chair that provides firm support or even on the floor. If this is uncomfortable for you, however, a reclining chair is another option. You can also try lying in bed or on the couch, although you might find yourself drifting off to sleep this way.

- **Attitude—** There is no right or wrong way to call up the relaxation response. The best approach is the one that works for you. If one time, place, or position doesn't turn out to be practical, try another one. Don't expect anything too dramatic. Otherwise, you'll just create more stress for yourself if you fail to live up to your own high expectations. Just let the experience unfold, and notice how you feel before, during, and after relaxation.

For more details, see the instructions for the Relaxation Response exercise in Chapter 11, on page 130.

The other R word

In the short run, these steps can help you to rest and relax. In the long run, they may also translate into another important benefit: resilience.

Psychologists define resilience as the process of adapting well to hardship, trauma, and other significant sources of ongoing stress—for example, family or marital conflicts, serious health problems, and work or financial pressures. In everyday terms, it's the ability to bounce back from difficult experiences and not only survive, but thrive.

Research has shown that resilience is the rule rather than the exception in most situations. All in all, we humans are pretty adaptable and hardy creatures. Nevertheless, everyone feels overwhelmed and underprepared from time to time. In such situations, several factors can bolster a person's natural resilience:

- A positive self-concept and firm belief in your own abilities.

- Mutually supportive relationships with family and friends.

- Good communication and problem-solving strategies.

- The capacity to understand and manage strong feelings and impulses.

- The ability to make realistic plans and take steps to carry them out.

- Last but definitely not least, good stress control skills.

Resilience isn't a trait you either have or don't have. Instead, it's a skill that can be learned and improved with practice. As you explore the stress management techniques in this book, you'll also be building your resilience. Ultimately, such techniques can make the difference between succumbing to chronic stress and coping successfully with the hard knocks that are an inevitable part of life.

Are we there yet?

Besides deep breathing and meditation, several other techniques—including progressive muscle relaxation, imagery, and yoga—can be used to call up the relaxation response. How can you tell when you've entered this state of deep relaxation? You'll notice that your breathing has slowed, and you may be aware that your heart rate has slowed down, too. Your muscles will feel less tight and tense, and some tension-related aches and soreness may vanish by the end of your relaxation session. Some people also experience a sensation of warmth in their hands and feet.

By the end of a single session, you should feel relaxed and calm, yet more alert and less tired than before. After practicing the relaxation response regularly for several weeks, you should start to feel a greater sense of control over your life. You may not be able to control the stock market, the next presidential election, or even your teenage child's behavior. However, you can manage your own response to these situations. Psychologically, just knowing that you have this power may increase your feeling of self-efficacy, the belief in your own ability to handle a situation capably. Physically, being able to elicit the relaxation response at will gives you a way to stop stress in its tracks, thereby decreasing your risk of stress-related illness.

You may notice a little improvement right away. As with anything else, however, big changes take time. From day to day, the changes may be so subtle that they're hard for you to see. However, you'll know you're getting somewhere when other people start commenting on your less-stressed demeanor. If you want more proof, try using some of the techniques in this book every day for six weeks. Then go back and repeat the Self-Test assessments. When you compare your scores now to those you got earlier, you may see that you have indeed come a long way.

3: The Seven Tactics

Chances are, you picked up this book because you're at least thinking about making changes to reduce the stress in your life. Before you embark on this path, it makes sense to think about the steps you've already taken to control stress. Some of us are naturals at stress management, and others are not. However, we've all developed our own habitual ways of dealing with stressful situations.

Not all of these habits are good ones. Some people try to keep stress at bay by feeding their addictions to alcohol, drugs, cigarettes, food, sex, gambling, or overspending. Others lash out at those around them, becoming verbally or even physically abusive. And still others just suffer in quiet desperation. In the long run, such counterproductive behaviors only lead to more stress, not less.

In contrast, the best stress managers tend to use more effective coping skills. They make relaxation a habit, and they know how to balance work and play. This doesn't automatically mean that they're less ambitious or successful than their hard-driving peers, however. On the

contrary, with the mind cleared of fruitless anxiety and worry, it may be possible for them to concentrate more intently on the important stuff. Research has shown that reduced stress often translates into increased productivity and creativity. It really is possible to de-stress for success.

Hardy in hard times

One psychologist who has studied stress coping skills is Suzanne Kobasa, PhD. As the story goes, when Kobasa was still a graduate student, she had a revelation while flipping through a magazine in a waiting room. She came across a stress quiz, and, when she tallied up her score, she found that it placed her in the danger zone for illness—yet she was fine. Kobasa reasoned that there must be protective factors that allow some people to get through difficult times relatively unscathed.

In the 1970s, Kobasa and her colleagues put her intuition to the test by studying a group of executives. They found that certain individuals were, indeed, unusually resistant to the health-eroding effects of stress. Kobasa used the term "stress-hardy" to describe these individuals. She found that they tended to share three core characteristics, nicknamed the three C's:

- **Commitment—** The stress-hardy executives were actively engaged by whatever was happening around them. They were also intrigued by other people, and they found meaning in their work and personal lives. According to Kobasa, such commitment can be seen as the opposite of alienation and withdrawal.

- **Control—** The stress-hardy executives believed that they could influence events in their lives. They were also willing to act on these beliefs rather than be victims of circumstance. This characteristic can be seen as the opposite of helplessness.

- **Challenge**— The stress-hardy types viewed life demands as challenges rather than threats. They also saw change as an opportunity for personal growth. This is the exact opposite of stress-prone types, who tend to see threats around every corner.

Kobasa had uncovered a profound truth: Challenges are positive and invigorating, while threats are negative and stressful—and the same situation can often be interpreted either way, depending on a person's habitual thinking style.

C is for coping

One way of assessing your own coping style is by asking yourself how closely it matches Kobasa's three Cs:

- Are you actively involved in your work, family life, and community? Or do you keep life at arm's length?

- Do you feel as if you have the power to influence events around you? Or do you see yourself as powerless?

- Do you view change as a challenge to be met with expected success? Or does the very thought of change send you into a panic?

If you chose the second option in any of the above pairs, you may not be enjoying the health benefits of stress hardiness. But there's also good news: The very act of trying out new stress control methods may bring about some positive changes in your attitude. It's harder to feel disengaged when you're trying something new and interesting. It's harder to feel powerless when you're learning tactics for taking charge of your own stress. And it's easier to accept change calmly once you've learned to call up the relaxation response whenever you need it.

Seven paths, one destination

The three Cs are beneficial characteristics that you might want to work toward. However, even if you're not the stress-hardy type, you don't have to change your whole personality before you can start reducing stress. There are as many different ways of handling stress as there are stressed-out individuals in the world. Given enough time and patience, you're bound to find one that works for you. The most popular approaches can be grouped into seven broad categories.

- **Tactic 1**— Focusing your mind intently to bring on the relaxation response. For example:
- Deep breathing
- Meditation
- Mindfulness meditation
- Body scan
- Progressive muscle relaxation

- **Tactic 2**— Redefining the situation mentally so it is no longer viewed as threatening. For example:
- Cognitive reframing
- Affirmations
- Thought stopping
- Humor
- Imagery

- **Tactic 3**— Using Eastern methods to restore your mental and physical balance. For example:
- Qigong
- T'ai chi
- Acupressure
- Shiatsu

- **Tactic 4**— Using yoga methods to calm your mind and relax your body. For example:
- Hatha yoga
- Yoga breathing
- Mantra meditation

- **Tactic 5**— Relieving muscle tension through exercise and massage. For example:
- Stretching
- Aerobic exercise
- Swedish massage
- Reflexology
- Indian head massage

- **Tactic 6**— Filling your mind with perceptions of pleasure rather than threat. For example:
- Aromatherapy
- Music
- Nature
- Social support
- Spirituality

- **Tactic 7**— Using coping strategies that stop stress before it starts. For example:
- Time management
- Communication
- Assertiveness
- Goal setting

We'll look at each of these tactics in turn in the next seven chapters. At first, some of the approaches will surely seem more familiar or natural to you than others. By all means, try the approaches that appeal to you right off the bat. However, you might want to sample a few of the others as well. You may be pleasantly surprised to discover how well they fit once you try them on.

Dear diary

Once you begin your stress control program, you may find it helpful to keep a diary of the approaches you've tried and the results you've achieved. The diary itself can serve as a handy reminder to de-stress, and the very act of writing about your efforts can help focus them. If you hit a roadblock, looking back through the diary can help you identify strategies that worked well in the past.

Please note:

As you read more about the tactics, you'll notice that many have been shown in scientific studies to help control not only stress, but also the symptoms of various diseases. This doesn't mean the tactics can treat or cure a disease on their own, however. Mind/body techniques such as the ones described in this book are meant to be a complement to, not a replacement for, standard medical care.

Below is an example of a daily diary form. For Stress Level, rate your stress from 1 (for extremely relaxed) to 10 (for extremely tense).

Today's Date:	Method 1:	Method 2:	Method 3:
Time Started			
Stress Level at Start			
Time Ended			
Stress Level at End			
Notes on Progress			
Notes on Obstacles			

Staying on course

The road to health is paved with good intentions. But, no matter how noble your intentions may be, you'll undoubtedly run into a few potholes on the way to less stress. One common problem is staying motivated for the long haul. Think about how much easier most people find it to stick to a diet once they've joined a support group or to go to the gym once they've found a workout buddy. The same principle holds true for sticking to a stress control plan. Taking turns giving massages with your spouse or signing up for a yoga class with a friend is a great way to keep up your motivation. Plus, spending time with family and friends has been shown to be a potent stress reliever in its own right.

Be careful, though, not to judge yourself by someone else's yardstick. If your next-door neighbor swears by acupressure, but you don't find it as helpful, that's okay. No two people are the same when it comes to stress relief. Instead of a one-size-fits-all solution, you need a stress control plan that's tailor-made for your individual preferences, circumstances, lifestyle, and personality. Otherwise, you're less likely to make your new stress reduction skills a permanent part of your life.

If you have trouble finding time to practice a particular relaxation technique, write it on your calendar the same way you would a business meeting or a date with a friend. By setting aside a specific block of time for your practice, you make a commitment to yourself to actually do it. You might also get up a few minutes earlier each morning to start the day off right with a relaxation session.

Finally, don't expect to become the guru of calm overnight. It took you years to learn your current stress coping habits. While it won't take years to unlearn them, it certainly will require more than a couple of days. Don't set yourself up for frustration by expecting an instant transformation. Instead, pay attention to small changes in how you feel. Be assured that, in time, those small changes can add up to big improvements in your mental and physical well-being.

4: Breathing and Meditation

Tactic: Focusing your mind intently to bring on the relaxation response.

The body comes readymade with a mechanism for turning off stress. Known as the relaxation response, this mechanism reverses the physiological changes that stress causes. Heart rate, blood pressure, breathing rate, muscle tension, and metabolism all decrease. While there are many ways to activate the relaxation response, two of the simplest are focused deep breathing and basic meditation. Other methods discussed in this chapter include mindfulness

meditation, which is rooted in Zen Buddhist practices, and the body scan, a full-body relaxation technique that uses mindfulness. Finally, the chapter will conclude with progressive muscle relaxation, another full-body technique that is widely taught by medical centers around the country.

Deep breathing

Imagine yourself driving down the freeway when a semi-truck suddenly cuts in front of you, forcing you to slam on your brakes and swerve to avert an accident. A minute later, you're safe but still shaken. You need to collect yourself in order to continue driving safely. What do you do? If you're like most of us, you'll take a couple of deep breaths to calm down. You instinctively know to breathe deeply when you need to relax in a hurry.

Most of the time, you probably take breathing for granted. Yet with each breath in, you're nourishing your body, and with each breath out, you're helping rid it of wastes. Here's what happens: When you breathe air into your lungs, it passes through a series of branching tubes until it finally ends up in tiny air sacs called alveoli. These sacs are covered with a mesh of very small, thin-walled blood vessels called capillaries. Oxygen passes through the sac walls and into the capillaries, where it enters the bloodstream. The blood then circulates throughout the body, bringing life-giving oxygen to all the cells. Through a process called cellular respiration, the cells use this oxygen to produce energy. The blood then picks up carbon dioxide and other wastes and carries them back to the lungs, where they're expelled when you breathe out.

Of course, all of this occurs quite automatically. However, you can become more aware of your breathing with practice. As you do, you'll notice that there are different breathing styles. Most adults rely mainly on shallow chest breathing, in which the chest expands with each breath in and contracts with each breath out. This is also the way people naturally breathe when under stress. The more stressed out you are, the more shallow, rapid, and irregular your breathing is likely to become. You may fail to breathe out completely in your

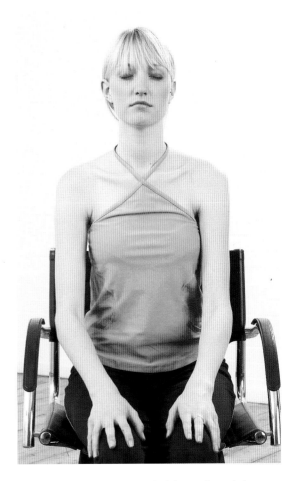

rush to get air, or you may hold your breath for several seconds. Think about feeling "breathless tension" or "holding your breath" in fearful anticipation. Either way, your breathing may become constricted, which can lead to panicky feelings of shortness of breath or chest tightness.

Contrast this to deep belly breathing. Since air is drawn down deeper into the lungs, it is the abdomen, rather than the chest, that rises with each breath in and falls with each breath out. This is the way babies and children usually breathe. For anyone of any age, it leads to a more efficient exchange of oxygen and carbon dioxide than chest breathing. By shifting to deeper, slower, more regular breathing, you can also gain some control over the constricted, anxious feelings that are associated with stress. Your body and your mind just naturally feel more relaxed.

41

Breathing lessons

To make deep breathing even more effective, it helps to focus intently on the rhythmic pattern of your breath as it goes in and out. You'll breathe easier—both literally and figuratively—once you get the knack of focused deep breathing. This skill is not only a marvelous stress reliever in itself, but also the first step in many other relaxation techniques. These are the basic steps:

1. Sit in a comfortable position.

2. Close your eyes. Place one hand on your belly, just below the navel (see above right picture).

3. Take a long, deep breath in. Try to make your hand rise slightly as you inhale (see below right picture).

4. Let the breath out slowly. Try to feel your hand fall slightly as you exhale.

5. Keep taking slow, deep, even breaths for a few minutes. Focus on the steady rising and falling of your hand.

If you have trouble getting the hang of belly breathing at the outset, try lying down and placing a book (instead of your hand) on your belly. Then concentrate on making the book move up and down with your breathing. Many people find that the visual cue helps at first. Once you've mastered deep breathing, though, you'll be able to do it anytime, anywhere, in any position.

Meditation

In some circles, meditation has an undeserved reputation for being esoteric and difficult to learn. In fact, it's really nothing more complicated than the practice of focusing your mind intently on

a particular thing or activity, while becoming relatively oblivious to everything else. The deep breathing method described above could be considered a basic form of meditation with your own breath as the focus point. The mantra meditation used by yoga practitioners and many other meditators is another form that places the focus on a special sound or word, called a mantra. If sitting quietly isn't your cup of tea, you can also combine meditation with a gentle, rhythmic activity, such as walking or t'ai chi.

To understand why meditation is so helpful, try closing your eyes for a few minutes and paying close attention to your thoughts. You may be surprised by how active your mind really is. Whether you're thinking about the grocery list, recalling the argument you had with your spouse last night, or fantasizing about the car you'll buy when you win the lottery, chances are your mind is always on the go.

All this thinking, thinking, thinking can be quite exhausting. It also makes it hard to mentally slow down long enough to focus on anything for more than a few seconds at a time.

Meditation offers a brief sabbatical from the busyness of thinking. Recent research using sophisticated brain-imaging technology is giving scientists a fascinating glimpse at precisely how this occurs. In one study, researchers at the University of Pennsylvania hooked up meditators to IVs containing a special dye. They also placed a long string next to each meditator. The string was snaked across the room and under a door to an adjacent room, where the other end was tied to a researcher's finger. When the meditator reached a state of deep relaxation, he or she pulled the string, and the researcher released the dye into the meditator's arm. The dye then traveled through the person's bloodstream until it reached the brain, where it was absorbed in higher concentrations by areas that were more active. The differences in activity could then be seen in images of the brain.

This study showed that the brain doesn't shut off during meditation, but does block out some information that it would normally let in. Specifically, it blocks information from reaching the parietal lobe, part of the brain that processes sensory data about the outside world. Other studies have likewise found big differences between the meditative state and the ordinary

waking state, both in the areas of the brain that are active and the brain waves that are produced. If the process is repeated often enough, the nerve cells in the brain adapt to the meditative state. At this point, the brain has actually retrained itself to function in a new way.

Numerous studies have documented the power of meditation to affect the rest of the body as well. Researchers have found that meditation can produce changes in immune function and blood pressure that may have important implications for health. Meditation has also been shown to improve the quality of life for people with a wide range of medical conditions, including breast cancer, prostate cancer, psoriasis, fibromyalgia, chronic pain, and anxiety disorders.

In addition, meditation has a long tradition of being used to enhance spiritual or personal growth. In fact, the word meditation comes from the Sanskrit *medha*, which can be translated as "doing the wisdom." People who use meditation for spiritual purposes typically do some focused deep breathing first to get into a calm, receptive frame of mind. Then, while still in the meditative state, they reflect on a certain experience, issue, or

43

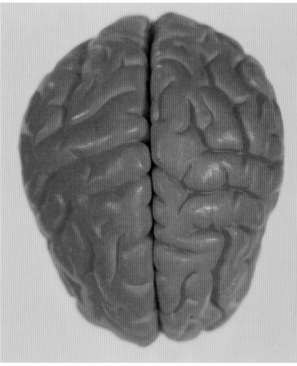

spiritual truth in order to gain greater insight into it. Of course, it's also quite possible to meditate strictly for the health benefits, with no spiritual intentions at all. Either approach is equally valid, depending on your goals.

Your brain on meditation

Meditation is an ancient practice, but the technology to peer inside the meditating brain is a new development. Research using the latest brain-imaging technology has found that meditation may calm the mind by quieting most regions of the brain. One study was conducted by Herbert Benson, MD, the cardiologist who named the relaxation response, and his colleagues. The participants were Sikhs who meditated regularly. Before the study started, all the participants practiced meditating under less-than-quiet conditions. During the study itself, they were placed inside a clanking functional MRI scanner, the machine that mapped their brain activity, while technicians and researchers milled about. In many ways, the distractions weren't that different from those you might encounter trying to meditate in an office or public park.

As expected, the scans showed that most areas of the participants' brains were much less active than what is normally seen during a waking state. However, a few regions of the brain became more active than normal. Among these regions were the limbic system and brain stem, parts of the brain involved in expressing emotion and regulating bodily functions such as heart rate and breathing rate. Some other isolated areas of the brain—especially those involved in attention—also became extremely active. So while most brain functions were muted during meditation, a few were heightened, a paradox Benson calls "calm commotion."

Counting to 10

A full-blown meditation session typically lasts at least 20 minutes. However, you can get a smaller taste of the experience by practicing this mini-meditation. It's based on the old adage that you should count to 10 when you get upset. It turns out that this advice really works if you focus intently on the counting. Here is a variation to try the next time you need to calm down quickly:

1. Take a few long, deep breaths to relax. Focus on the breath going in and out. (see above right picture).

2. Imagine yourself in an elevator at the top of a 10-story office building. Breathe in deeply. Then silently say the number 10 as you breathe out.

3. Continue counting backward from 10 to 1 this way as you mentally ride the elevator down from the top floor to the bottom.

With each passing floor, feel yourself sinking deeper and deeper into relaxation (see below right picture).

For longer meditation sessions, see the following exercises in Chapter 11: the sitting meditation, the walking meditation, and the meditation on friendship.

Mini-meditations

The following are three more mini-meditations that you can use when you need to relax fast.

Air conditioning

1. Breathe in slowly through your nose. Focus on your breath, and notice how cool the air feels coming in.

2. Breathe out slowly through your mouth. Focus on your breath, and notice how much warmer the air feels going out.

3. Repeat several times.

Spelling bee

1. Take a few long, deep breaths to relax. Focus on the breath going in and out.

2. Begin silently spelling your first name, saying one letter to yourself on each exhalation.

3. Ask yourself how you feel when you get to the last letter. If you're still tense, begin spelling your middle name. And if you're still tense after that, go on to your last name.

Bliss list

1. This approach was suggested by Peg Baim, NP, MS, clinical director of training at the Mind/Body Medical Institute in Boston. Make a list of images or ideas that cause you to feel inspiration, appreciation, or an awareness of beauty. These are three factors that can shift your mindset in a more positive direction.

2. When you're feeling stressed, take a few long, deep breaths to relax. Then choose an image or idea from the list, and contemplate it for a few minutes.

Mindfulness meditation

Mindfulness is another variation on the meditation theme. In essence, this Zen Buddhist practice involves fully focusing your attention on whatever you're experiencing from moment to moment. Think of it this way: Ordinary attention is like a flashlight illuminating a fairly large area, but often none too brightly. Mindfulness is like a laser pointer, shining very intensely on one miniscule spot.

To see how this works, take a few minutes to be mindful of the sounds around you. Concentrate all your attention on the sounds, but don't strain to hear them or attempt to

Body scan

analyze them. Instead, try to regard them as pure sounds without any particular meaning attached. For example, if a phone rings, notice the tone, but don't try to guess who might be on the other end. Notice the silences between the sounds as well. If your mind starts to wander away, gently guide it back.

You can use mindfulness as a formal meditation technique. However, you can also use it to become more fully aware of your experiences in everyday life. The idea is to take note of your experience here and now without judging or reacting to it. In short, you become a keen observer of your present state of mind. In the process, you may find yourself stressing less about what happened yesterday or might happen tomorrow.

For an example of mindfulness in action, see Mindful Eating in Chapter 11.

Mindfulness-based stress reduction programs are now offered by many medical centers and hospitals. A number of these are modeled on a program first developed by Jon Kabat-Zinn, PhD, at the University of Massachusetts Medical Center. Kabat-Zinn knew that accepting your body just as it is can be hard for people with body image issues, not to mention those with illness or pain. To foster such acceptance, he suggested a mindfulness-based practice known as a body scan. It can be used by anyone who wants to get in closer touch with his or her body while inducing a state of deep relaxation.

Essentially, a body scan entails focusing attention on one part of your body after another while noticing and accepting nonjudgmentally how you feel at the moment. Many people find that it helps

to have a recording guide them through the process. That way, if their attention wanders, the voice on the tape can lead them back to the scan. If you make your own recording, remember to allow plenty of time between the steps. It takes about 20 to 30 minutes for most people to complete a full-body scan. For detailed instructions, see the Body Scan in Chapter 11.

Progressive muscle relaxation

Progressive muscle relaxation is another full-body technique that has proven to be quite helpful for many people. It was developed in the 1920s by Edmund Jacobson as a way of addressing the muscle tension that goes along with stress and anxiety. The technique involves systematically tensing and relaxing all the major muscle groups of the body in turn. While doing this, you focus intently on the feelings associated with tension and relaxation. That way, you may become more attuned to muscle tension when it occurs at other times throughout the day. The sooner you recognize this early warning sign of stress, the more quickly you can begin to counteract it by taking some deep breaths or doing a mini-meditation on the spot.

Tensing the muscles before relaxing them serves another function as well. You need to maintain a certain amount of tension in everyday life in order to hold your body upright. During progressive muscle relaxation, though, you want to reduce your muscle tension below that everyday level. Tightening the muscles creates a momentum that makes it easier to loosen them afterward. It's like a pendulum that swings first above the normal tension level and then below it.

Isolating specific muscle groups this way can take a bit of practice. The first few times you try progressive muscle relaxation, you may not feel completely relaxed afterward. However, most people get the hang of the technique after a week or two of daily practice. If a particular muscle group is giving you trouble, it may help to practice tensing and relaxing that group alone occasionally throughout the day. The effort can be well worth it. Excellent results have been achieved using progressive muscle relaxation to reduce stress and

other symptoms associated with conditions such as neck and back pain, muscle spasms, high blood pressure, irritable bowel syndrome, anxiety, depression, chronic fatigue, and insomnia.

Care should be taken not to squeeze your muscles too hard, however. All you need to do is tighten the muscles enough to feel a contrast with the relaxed state. You shouldn't feel any pain, discomfort, or cramping. If you do get a cramp, release that muscle group immediately, and be careful not to tense so hard next time. Be especially cautious about excessive tightening of the back or neck. If you have an injury, check with your physician before trying this technique.

For more details, see the Progressive Muscle Relaxation exercise in Chapter 11.

your quality of life. Another big plus to these techniques is that they are extremely low risk. It's hard to imagine anything much safer than sitting quietly and breathing deeply. Occasionally, though, people who are just getting started with the breathing exercises wind up feeling dizzy. If this happens to you, let your breathing return to normal, and take a few minutes to regain your balance before trying to stand up.

Meditation can tap into powerful unconscious thoughts and emotions. Most often, this leads to feelings of enhanced well-being and calmness, but it can sometimes bring up disturbing feelings. If you find yourself inexplicably angry, anxious, or sad while meditating, try to notice the feelings without attempting to make sense of them. Then gently guide your mind back to your focus point. If this doesn't work and the feeling is very upsetting, however, you may want to choose another relaxation technique. The goal, after all, is to end up feeling less stressed, not more so.

Many people teach themselves to meditate. Others, however, prefer to join a class. It's a good way to make friends with similar interests, and the social support from fellow meditators can be very motivational. Just keep in mind that this type of instruction isn't licensed or certified on a national level. Meditation is taught by people from diverse backgrounds at meditation, yoga, and religious centers as well as medical clinics, hospitals, and mental health facilities. When choosing an instructor, let your common sense be your guide. Visit a class before signing up. If a particular approach makes you feel uneasy, look for one that's a better match. There's always another approach to try, so keep searching until you find one that really fits.

Focal points

The great thing about techniques that rely on mental focus to reduce stress is that they can be used by almost anyone. You don't have to be spiritually motivated or New Age-y. The techniques are adaptable to a wide range of personal interests and personality styles. They are also flexible enough to fit into just about any schedule. For maximum results, most experts recommend that you practice deep breathing or meditation for at least 20 minutes once or twice a day. While this might be nice, it isn't always realistic. If you're pressed for time, you can shorten a deep breathing or meditation session as much as necessary. In fact, some brief breathing exercises and mini-meditations can be performed in as little as two or three minutes. The benefits from shorter sessions may not be as dramatic as those from longer ones, but they can still make a noticeable difference in

5: Mental Approaches

Tactic: Redefining the situation mentally so it is no longer viewed as threatening.

Stress is a physiological response, but it begins with a psychological reaction. Your mind perceives a situation as a threat that you're unprepared to handle, and suddenly your body shifts into overdrive. The good news is that what starts in your mind can end there, too. That's the basic premise behind mental approaches—they help you redefine a situation so that it is no longer viewed as threatening. One widely used approach is cognitive reframing, which is similar to "positive thinking." It typically involves identifying unrealistically negative thoughts and replacing them with more realistically positive ones. Other popular techniques include affirmations, which are brief statements of self-encouragement, and thought stopping, which is a method for controlling worry. Finally, the power of the mind can also be harnessed through the use of humor and imagination.

Cognitive reframing

Almost every waking minute of every day, you are engaged in a lively mental conversation with yourself. Much of this self-talk is so fleeting and automatic that you're barely aware of it. But it's there, whether you realize it or not, and it can have a big impact on your feelings and behavior. If the things you tell yourself are accurate, even if they're sometimes unpleasant truths, they help you get along. On the other hand, if you tell yourself half-truths and lies, you're not able to adapt appropriately to the real facts of a situation. Distorted thinking can take different forms. However, many of us get into a bad habit of looking at the world through mud-colored glasses. Our thoughts are often unrealistically helpless or hopeless, which leads to less-than-helpful behavior. Such thinking can also create unnecessary stress if benign situations are perceived as threats.

Imagine that you are meeting a friend for lunch at noon. By 12:10, your friend still hasn't arrived, and she hasn't called

to explain her tardiness. The rational response to this situation depends on what you know about the circumstances and your friend's past behavior. A realistic reaction might be to think, "She's probably tied up with a client," "She may be stuck in traffic without her phone," or, "She was 15 minutes late last time. She'll probably walk in the door any minute."

If you tend to be unrealistically negative, however, you're probably already thinking, "She's going to stand me up, " "She never liked me anyway," or "I just know there has been an accident. She might be lying dead on the side of the road right now." Obviously, the latter set of responses is going to create considerably more stress for you than the first set.

The way you interpret the situation will, in turn, affect your behavior. By the time your friend breezes into the restaurant five minutes later, you're apt to be in a lousy mood if you've just spent five minutes obsessing about her presumed treachery or possible demise. Lunch is likely to get off to a rocky start. On the other hand, if you've been passing the time calmly with a less alarmist attitude, you're more likely to greet your friend warmly and actually enjoy your meal together.

Cognitive reframing is based on the notion that you can eliminate or reduce a lot of stress by first identifying unrealistic thoughts and then restating them in more realistic terms. While this may sound like common sense, it wasn't developed as a structured psychotherapeutic technique until the

1950s, when Albert Ellis, PhD, introduced what is now known as rational emotive behavior therapy. Today, this is one of many varieties of cognitive-behavioral therapy, all of which aim to change the maladaptive thoughts and behaviors that are contributing to your current problems. According to Ellis, the steps to warding off unnecessary stress can be as simple as ABC:

- **Activators**— These are the facts and events that exist in your world. In the example of the late lunch, the activating event is your friend's tardiness.

- **Beliefs**— These are beliefs and attitudes about the situation. For example, you might believe that your friend is intentionally late because she doesn't like you.

- **Consequences**— These are emotions and behaviors that result from the beliefs. If the beliefs are faulty, the resulting emotions and behaviors are likely to be inappropriate and self-defeating as well. For example, if you believe that your friend's tardiness is intentional, you may feel quite stressed out and angry, and you may give your friend the cold shoulder when she arrives. Even if she has a good explanation for being late, you may not be open to hearing it by that point. Your lunch is apt to be ruined—not by your friend's lateness, but by your own inaccurate beliefs leading to inappropriate stress and hostile behavior.

Simply put, A doesn't lead directly to C. A leads to B, which leads to C—and the good news is that B is under your control. By changing your illogical beliefs, you can often change the consequences to make them more beneficial.

Minding your thoughts

There's a catch, however: It can be trickier than it sounds to identify the flaws in your own beliefs. Many irrational thoughts become so habitual that you barely notice them anymore. Such thoughts also tend to be couched in a fleeting mental shorthand, which makes them even harder to pin down. It takes conscious effort to become more aware of your thinking patterns. It can be done, however, with a little practice.

One thing that helps is being alert for common thinking errors. Most of us are guilty of these kinds of distortions at times:

- **Awfulizing**— Making a mountain out of a molehill. You start with an everyday problem and exaggerate it into a full-scale catastrophe. For example, you miss one meeting at work, and you think, "This is a disaster. I'm going to be fired."

- **Shouldizing**— Setting up unrealistic expectations about what "should," "must," or "ought to" happen. You inevitably feel let down, angry, frustrated, or guilty when real life doesn't work out that way. For example, you tell yourself, "I should own a luxury car," and then you feel frustrated when you can't afford it.

- **Overgeneralizing**— Thinking in black-or-white absolutes. You start with a relatively narrow fact and turn it into an overly broad rule about what "always" or "never" happens. For example, a relationship ends in a breakup, and you think, "I'm never going to find love."

- **Personalizing**— Blaming yourself for events beyond your control. For example, your spouse comes home from work cranky and stressed out, and you tell yourself, "It must be my fault."

Once you start noticing these kinds of errors in your thinking, you can begin correcting them. Unrealistically negative thoughts can be replaced with more realistically positive ones. Take the example where you missed one meeting at work. Instead of thinking, "This is a disaster," you might tell yourself, "I made a mistake. I'm usually on top of things, though. Most of the time, I'm very dependable"—assuming all of these statements are true, of course. You've just redefined the situation so that it's much less threatening. Since you no longer expect to be fired, your stress level stays low.

One caution: The new, more positive thoughts need to be firmly grounded in reality. If you've already missed four other meetings in the past month, there may be good reason for thinking you'll be fired. The idea is to look at the situation more accurately and honestly, whatever the truth may be. However, as a practical matter, it's usually overly negative, rather than overly positive, thoughts that lead to unnecessary stress.

For help getting started, see the Reframing Journal on the following page and the accompanying exercise in Chapter 11.

Same picture, new frame

This chart offers a few examples of cognitive reframing in action.

	Activator	Belief	Consequence	Disputation	New Consequence
Description	The event that set things in motion.	Your unrealistically negative belief about the situation.	The stress and inappropriate behaviors that result from your belief.	The more realistic belief with which you dispute the unrealistic one.	The more appropriate response that may result from your revised belief.
Example 1	You discover that you gained three pounds on vacation.	"This is terrible. My diet is shot now."	You feel stressed and depressed. You overeat in a vain attempt to feel better.	"I can get back on a healthy diet now. I'll lose those pounds in a couple of weeks."	You feel motivated to resume your diet. You soon shed the extra pounds.
Example 2	Your teenage son gets angry and yells an obscenity.	"I'm the parent. He should be more respect-ful."	You feel stressed and angry. You yell back, and your son storms out of the room.	"My son respects me. He just needs to learn how to control his temper."	You stay calm, serving as a good role model for your son.
Example 3	You are turned down for a promo-tion at work.	"It's all over. I'll never go anywhere in my career."	You feel stressed and unmotivated. Over the next several weeks, your perform-ance at work slacks off.	"I'm good at my job. I'll get ahead eventually, here or at another company."	You feel moti-vated to turn a setback into a comeback. You redouble your efforts at work.
Example 4	You are giving a talk when you notice two people in the audience laughing.	"I must have said some-thing stupid. I'm a lousy speaker."	You feel stressed. You lose track of what you're saying and stumble through the speech.	"I don't know what they're laughing at, but it proba-bly has nothing to do with me."	You stay focused on your speech, enabling you to give it your best effort.

Affirmations

In addition to replacing irrationally negative thoughts, you can make a conscious effort to add more positive ones. Affirmations are brief, self-encouraging statements that have special meaning for you. These little booster shots of positive thinking can lift your spirits and motivate you to take constructive action. When combined with reframing, they may help immunize you against senseless stress. These are the basic steps to follow:

1. Pick a recurring situation that is causing stress. Decide how you would ideally like to feel or behave in this situation.

2. Translate this goal into a short, personally-meaningful, positive statement starting with the words "I can" or "I am." Avoid using the word "not." For example, your statement might be "I can do the job" or "I am smart and capable."

3. Put your statement to the truth test. Does it reflect who you really are or what you can do? If not, tweak the statement to make it more realistically encouraging. For example, it won't help to tell yourself "I am young" when you're not. However, it might be perfectly accurate to think "I am youthful and energetic."

4. Repeat the statement silently to yourself whenever the stressful situation arises. Also, try saying it a few times when you first wake up or right after you've taken several long, deep breaths to bring on relaxation. Your mind is especially receptive when it's calm.

Thought stopping

Have you ever noticed how worrisome thoughts have a way of sticking in your mind and refusing to let go? They're like those annoying advertising jingles that keep playing over and over in your brain. You want to shut them off, but you don't know how. It's for situations like this that psychotherapists have developed another powerful mental technique known as

thought stopping. In the 1950s, therapists such as Joseph Wolpe, MD, popularized the technique, and it has been a staple of stress control ever since.

The procedure is simple: First you identify the worrisome thoughts that are causing you unnecessary stress and monopolizing too much of your attention. When you notice yourself having these thoughts throughout the day, start by giving yourself two or three minutes to really wallow in the worry. If possible, use a timer to make sure you

don't go over your time limit. When the time is up, interrupt your thoughts by yelling, "Stop!" If that isn't practical, you can covertly pinch yourself even snap yourself with a rubber band that you wear loosely around your wrist for just such occasions. The idea is that this sudden action will be enough to interrupt the obsessive worries.

There are three theories about why this may work. One, the stop command may function as a punishment. Two, it may act as a distraction. Three, it may yank you out of your mental rut long enough for your mind to set off in a brand-new direction. Once you've taken the first step and interrupted a negative thought, it

may be easier to take the next step and substitute a more positive statement. For this reason, thought stopping is often combined with cognitive reframing.

Thought stopping has been shown to help control a variety of obsessive thoughts and anxiety disorders. Of course, not all worry is bad. At the right times and in the right amounts, worry can be a valuable motivator. However, when worry becomes uncontrollable, unrealistic, and unproductive, it starts to work against you. Thought stopping can be a useful tool in these situations.

For more details, see the Thought Stopping instructions in Chapter 11.

Therapeutic writing

Therapeutic writing is another way to get your worries out into the open and then dispense with them. Bruce Rabin, MD, PhD, medical director of the Healthy Lifestyle Program at the University of Pittsburgh Medical Center, recommends this procedure. He says it often leads to a dramatic reduction in stress.

1. Pick something that is bothering you as the topic for your writing. It can be a distressing event that occurred today, or it can be a problem that has plagued you for decades. Any issue of concern will work.

2. Find a quiet spot where you won't be disturbed. Then write about your topic continuously for 15 minutes. Although Rabin says that he's still unsure why, it seems to be important that you write your thoughts out by hand. Typing on a computer doesn't appear to have the same benefits. If you run out of new things to say, repeat what you've already written. Don't worry about spelling, grammar, or punctuation. Just get your thoughts on paper. Also, if you start crying, don't be alarmed. Rabin says this is a common reaction.

3. When your 15 minutes are up, tear up or shred the paper immediately. Discard it so that no one—not even you—will ever see what you wrote.

Humor

Humor is yet another powerful coping strategy. It's hard not to feel better after a laugh, even in the direst of circumstances. That's because humor is, at its core, an expression of joy, optimism, and a positive outlook. There is nothing like laughing in the face of adversity to minimize the sense of threat.

Studies have found physiological evidence for humor's stress-busting capacity. For example, researchers from Loma Linda University Medical Center in California have shown that "mirthful

laughter"—in other words, happy laughter as opposed to black humor or sarcasm—can reduce stress hormone levels and enhance immune function. At the same time, humor also combats stress on a psychological level by changing people's perceptions of an event. Think about all the times you've seen an argument averted because someone cracked a joke to defuse a tense situation.

When you're afraid, humor can knock a perceived threat down to more manageable size. When you're depressed, a little levity can help you regain your perspective. How can a situation be all bad when it makes you laugh?

All laughter is not created equal, however. Much of what passes for humor in our society is actually sarcasm, hostility, or prejudice in a thinly-veiled disguise.

This kind of humor has the potential to increase stress rather than decrease it. Everyone has a different opinion about what's funny and what's not, but stress-relieving humor tends to be uplifting and inclusive, not demeaning and divisive.

You don't have to be the life of the party or a natural joke-teller to use humor to your advantage. These are some ways to add more laughter to your life:

- Start a scrapbook for jotting down jokes and saving cartoons.

- Listen to recordings of your favorite comedian in the car.

- Read funny books—they're often much funnier than sitcoms.

- Remember a story that always makes you smile.

- Spend more time with people who love to laugh.

Imagery

One final way to keep stress at bay is by using the power of imagination. Imagery is a popular stress control technique in which you use your imagination to bring about changes in your thoughts, feelings, and physical responses. Another common name for this approach is visualization. However, imagery is actually the broader term. While visualization implies seeing something with your mind's eye, imagery can involve imagining through any of your senses, including hearing, smell, taste, and touch. You may also run across references to guided imagery, which simply means that another person or a voice on a recording leads you through an imagery session.

To see just how potent imagery can be, then try this quick exercise: Imagine cutting a big, bright yellow lemon in half. Then picture yourself placing the cut side of the lemon inside your mouth. Now squeeze the lemon, and feel the juice drench your tongue. Imagine the sour juice flooding your tastebuds. Did you start to salivate and pucker your lips as though it were real? It doesn't take long for a mental image to cause an actual physical response.

Imagery can be used to call up the relaxation response in much the same way as breathing exercises or meditation. Moreover, some people find that focusing on a soothing image helps keep their mind from wandering and makes the whole relaxation process more enjoyable. Research has shown that imagery can help relieve stress and reduce anxiety and depression. It can also help people manage various types of pain as well as the side effects of chemotherapy. In addition, some studies have suggested that regular use of imagery may lower blood pressure and enhance immune function.

All of us already know how to create mental imagery. We do it every time we daydream, fantasize, or remember. To practice imagery as a more structured stress management technique, start out by sitting quietly and taking a few deep breaths to relax, just as you would before meditation. Then mentally focus

Imagine stresslessness

Most of us have sensory preferences, and some people have trouble drawing upon their less-preferred senses at first. To determine which kinds of imagery are particularly powerful for you, try to imagine each of the following sensations in turn. Which ones are most evocative? In your imagery sessions, start with the types of sensations that are most accessible to you. Then gradually try to bring in the other senses.

- Sight of a grassy meadow

- Sight of a rainbow

- Sound of a babbling brook

- Sound of children laughing

- Smell of fresh-baked cookies

- Smell of blooming roses

- Taste of rich chocolate

- Taste of a juicy pear

- Feel of floating in air

- Feel of warm water

To see how you can build on your personal sensory preferences, try this quick imagery exercise. Choose an image that symbolizes stress for you. For example:

- Sight of the color red

- Screech of fingernails on a chalkboard

- Smell of ammonia

- Taste of castor oil

- Feel of tension on a tightened rope

on a safe and soothing scene. You can invent this scene from scratch or base it on a pleasant memory. For example, you might choose a cozy hideaway from childhood, a real-life scene that makes you feel calm and secure, or an imaginary place with a serene view.

Another option is having someone else lead you through a predetermined scene, the broad outlines of which are verbally sketched out for you. Whichever approach you choose, however, it helps to add as many personally meaningful details as possible. It also helps to make the scene more vivid by involving as many senses as you can. If you're imagining a beach scene, for instance, don't just see the sand and water. Also hear the crash of the waves and the cry of the seagulls. Feel the sand between your toes, smell the fresh sea air, and taste the salt on the breeze.

Imagery scripts—whether provided by an instructor, on a recording, or in a book such as this one—can be useful starting points. Keep in mind, however, that not every theme will be appropriate for you. Most people find a beach scene very relaxing. However, if you once had a close call with drowning, imagining a beach scene may have exactly the opposite effect. Let your own reactions be your guide. If you start to feel more stressed and anxious rather than less while practicing imagery, stop the session. Then try imagery on another day using a different scene.

Now close your eyes, take a few deep breaths, and focus on this image for a few minutes. Then gradually have the stressful image fade or transform into a more restful one. For example, the color red might fade to pink, or the screech of fingernails on a chalkboard might transform into the sound of violins playing. Spend several more minutes soaking up the pleasant sensations associated with this new image. At the same time, you might repeat an affirmation to yourself, such as "I can make stress fade" or "I am in charge of my stress."

For a longer imagery session, see the Safe Haven exercise in Chapter 11.

Mental notes

It's quite possible to train yourself to use the mental techniques presented in this chapter. However, many people find that they make faster progress with the help of an instructor or therapist. Guided imagery is taught by instructors from diverse backgrounds. Be sure you feel comfortable with a particular instructor's approach before signing up for a class or one-on-one sessions. If you plan to tackle deep emotional issues or relationship problems, look for an instructor who is also licensed as a mental health professional.

For more complex techniques, such as cognitive restructuring and thought stopping, an appropriately licensed and trained cognitive-behavioral therapist may be your best bet for professional guidance. Since there are several versions of cognitive-behavioral therapy practiced today, look for a therapist whose style and technique are well matched to your individual needs. As with other stress control techniques, the "right" method is the one that works for you.

Cognitive restructuring is all about putting your thoughts to the reality test. The same test should be applied to your expectations for mental stress control. Realistically, you're never going to eliminate all the stress in your life, and that's okay. Most people would rather deal with the ups and downs of daily life than become emotional zombies. However, mental techniques can help you control whether your emotional response is constructive or destructive. You don't have to start thinking like Pollyanna on Prozac, but a little less worry and a little more optimism, confidence, humor, and imagination can make even the worst situation seem less threatening.

6: Eastern Methods

Tactic: Using Eastern methods to restore your mental and physical balance.

Modern society doesn't have a monopoly on stress. Although the nature of stress may have changed over the centuries, its existence is a timeless and universal fact of life. It should come as no surprise, then, that ancient systems of Eastern health and healing include methods for relieving stress by restoring mental and physical balance. Qigong (pronounced "chee-GUNG") is a Chinese system of self-care that aims to balance the flow of qi (pronounced "chee"), or vital life energy. One of the best known forms of qigong is t'ai chi, an approach to exercise that's part martial art and part moving meditation. Qi is thought to flow along energy pathways within the body, and acupressure aims to stimulate specific points along those paths. Shiatsu (pronounced "shee-OT-soo") is a Japanese version of acupressure that's also based on the principle of balancing energy flow. The one thing all of these methods have in common is the belief that stress, disease, and injury disrupt the vital energy inside the body, while meditation, breathing exercises, movement, and massage help restore it.

Qigong

The concept of qi lies at the heart of traditional Chinese concepts of health and illness. Qi is believed to regulate mental, physical, emotional, and spiritual well-being. It's influenced by the opposing forces of yin, or negative energy, and yang, or positive energy. Qi is said to flow through the body along pathways called meridians, which are like rivers that irrigate the body and nourish its tissues. Any obstruction along one of the meridians is like a dam that blocks the vital energy flow, creating disease and dysfunction. The purpose of qigong is to prevent or remove any such blockages by balancing yin and yang. Qigong includes moving forms, which involve physical exercise, and still forms, which focus solely on meditation and breath control.

According to traditional Chinese philosophy, there are 12 primary and

eight secondary meridians within the body. Western scientists have found the existence of meridians hard to verify, since they don't correspond to nerve or circulatory pathways. Yet studies have found that approaches based on these elusive meridians do indeed seem to have beneficial effects. For example, a recent article in an American Medical Association journal analyzed 47 previous studies that had looked at the benefits of t'ai chi for people with chronic health conditions. The studies reported increased balance, flexibility, and cardiovascular health. In healthy individuals, the studies also reported decreased stress, anxiety, and pain.

The exercise component of qigong can take a variety of forms. While t'ai chi is the most familiar, you may also run into classes using other styles. In general, these other styles are less fluid than t'ai chi, and some are considerably more strenuous.

Others, however, are gentle and undemanding enough to be performed by people of all ages, fitness levels, and physical abilities. Some can even be done by people in wheelchairs or those who are bedridden. If you're thinking about joining a qigong class, your best bet is to talk to the instructor first and observe a few classes to get an idea of what's involved. Then, if you have any special health or mobility concerns, you can better judge if this particular class is appropriate for you.

Some Westerners who practice qigong firmly believe that meridians exist, perhaps in a still-unidentified network within the body's connective tissue. Others approach qigong strictly as an effective form of exercise or meditation that can be used to call up the relaxation response. Either way, this 3,000-year-old system seems to be as relevant as ever in the twenty-first century.

Quiet qigong

One essential skill taught by qigong is the ability to enter a quiet, meditative state of mind. As with other forms of meditation, this involves focusing the mind intently on one particular thing, while becoming relatively unaware of everything else. Among the focus points used in qigong meditation are:

- A point on the body. Most often, this is the *dan tien*, a point 1 to 3 inches below the navel, near the physical center of the body.

- A focus word or phrase. The person silently repeats the word or phrase in order to elicit the relaxation response and calm the mind.

- The feeling of breathing. The person focuses on the rhythmic rise and fall of the breath without straining too hard to control it.

- The act of counting. The person silently counts each breath until the ears hear nothing, the eyes see nothing, and the mind is quiet.

- The sound of breathing. The person aims to make the breath inaudible. By focusing on hearing what cannot be heard, the person enters a quiet state.

Another essential component of qigong is breath awareness. Different styles of breathing are used in qigong. These are some of the common ones:

- **Natural breathing**— A person's breathing style in the absence of conscious mental control. While effortless, it may not be very deep.

- **Abdominal breathing**— The familiar deep breathing style. The abdomen expands on each breath in and contracts on each breath out.

- **Reversed breathing**— The opposite of abdominal breathing. The abdomen contracts on each breath in and expands on each breath out.

To try a relaxing exercise that's intended to help you become more aware of qi, see the Quiet Qi Meditation in Chapter 11.

T'ai chi

The best known method of moving qigong is t'ai chi, which combines slow, flowing movements with a calm, alert state of mind. T'ai chi originated around the thirteenth century as a melding of martial arts and meditation. According to legend, a martial arts master was inspired by the sight of a crane and snake in battle. The snake successfully evaded the crane's sharp beak with its slow but supple movements. The master set out to develop a system of self-defense that was based not on brute force, but on grace and suppleness as well as the healthy flow of qi. Some modern teachers use

this story to impart a crucial lesson about stress. The moral: Being flexible in the face of change may produce better results than trying to resist it.

T'ai chi students begin by learning a series of slow, controlled movements, called a form. Each form is composed of 20 to 100-plus moves and takes from 8 to 20 or more minutes to complete. To properly balance yin and yang, each movement is paired with its opposite. For example, a turn to the right is paired with a turn to the left. The emphasis is on technique rather than strength or power. The resulting movements have the quality

Feng shui

of a fluid, slow-motion dance. While performing these choreographed movements, a person practices abdominal breathing. At the same time, meditative focus is centered on the *dan tien*—the body's center of gravity, and the point from which effortless movement is thought to emanate.

As a stress control method, t'ai chi has much to commend it. Many people find the combination of slow, graceful movement and intense mental focus to be very relaxing. Because the moves are so smooth, t'ai chi is also an especially gentle form of exercise. The benefits are enjoyed by millions of people worldwide, young and old alike. Studies have found positive mental and physical effects both for healthy individuals and for people with a wide range of medical conditions, including arthritis, high blood pressure, heart disease, and multiple sclerosis. If you have a condition that limits your ability to exercise, ask your doctor whether t'ai chi might be a good choice for you.

According to ancient Chinese traditions, qi is present not only in living things, but also in wind and water. Feng shui (pronounced "fung shway")—a term composed of the Chinese words for these two elements—is the art of designing environments in harmony with the flow of qi. Proponents claim that the proper placement of furniture, ornaments, rooms, buildings, and even towns can aid the beneficial flow of vital energy. On the other hand, the improper placement of manmade objects and structures is said to promote stress and disease. Scientifically speaking, there's no good evidence that using the principles of feng shui actually reduces stress or enhances well-being. However, if feng shui helps you create a living or working space that seems more harmonious, you'll undoubtedly feel more at ease there.

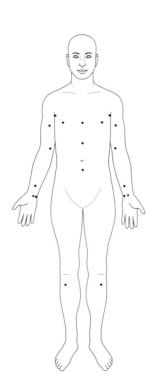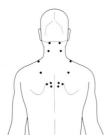

Main acupressure points

Acupressure

In traditional Chinese medicine, many ailments are treated by the stimulation of specific acupoints located on the meridians. More than 2,000 such points have been identified, each of which is supposed to affect particular organs or tissues via the meridian network. Perhaps the best known way of stimulating these points is needle acupuncture, which involves the insertion of hair-thin needles. However, another common method is acupressure, which involves applying pressure at particular sites with fingers or tools. Still other methods of stimulating the points include electrical impulses, heat, lasers, sound waves, friction, suction, and magnets.

Most scientific studies to date have involved needle acupuncture, although some have used acupressure or other related methods. Taken as a whole, the studies offer compelling evidence that acupuncture and its variations really do have the ability to affect health and wellness. A 2002 report by the World Health Organization lists 28 diseases, symptoms, or conditions for which acupuncture has been proved through controlled trials to be an effective treatment, and an additional 63 for which

the therapeutic effect of acupuncture has been shown, but for which further proof is needed. Two of the conditions on these lists are "competition stress syndrome" and depression. The others run the gamut from hay fever, high blood pressure, and obesity to insomnia, nausea, and various types of pain.

Western scientists still aren't sure exactly how acupuncture and its relatives may have their effects. When it comes to acupressure, one possible explanation is that it's simply a relaxing form of massage. In addition, a report from the U.S. National Center for Complementary and Alternative Medicine, part of the National Institutes of Health, notes evidence that acupuncture points may be strategic conductors of electromagnetic signals. Stimulating these points may enable electromagnetic signals within the body to be relayed at a faster rate than normal. These signals, in turn, may cause the release of brain chemicals, such as endorphins, that kill pain and produce feelings of well-being. The signals may also activate the immune system.

1.

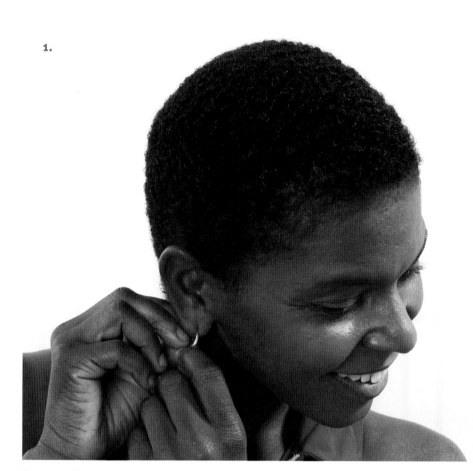

Ear points

Interestingly, one problem for which acupressure, as opposed to needles, has been tentatively shown to work is stress. The acupoint in question is located on the ear. This may explain why massaging the ears is so relaxing. Try it for yourself:

1. Remove any ear jewelry that may get in your way. Don't try this exercise if your ears are sore or infected. Then close your eyes, and grasp both earlobes between your thumbs and index fingers. Gently squeeze and pull the lobes downward. Take three deep breaths.

2. Move your thumbs and fingers a little higher up the outer edge of the earlobe. Lightly pinch, holding for a few seconds. Continue this way all the way up the outside of the ears.

3. When you get to the top of your ears, gently squeeze and pull the ears upward. Take three deep breaths.

4. Cup your ears lightly over your hands. Slowly stretch the ears by moving your hands forward and backward.

5. Keep your hands cupped over your ears. Continue breathing slowly and deeply for a few more minutes.

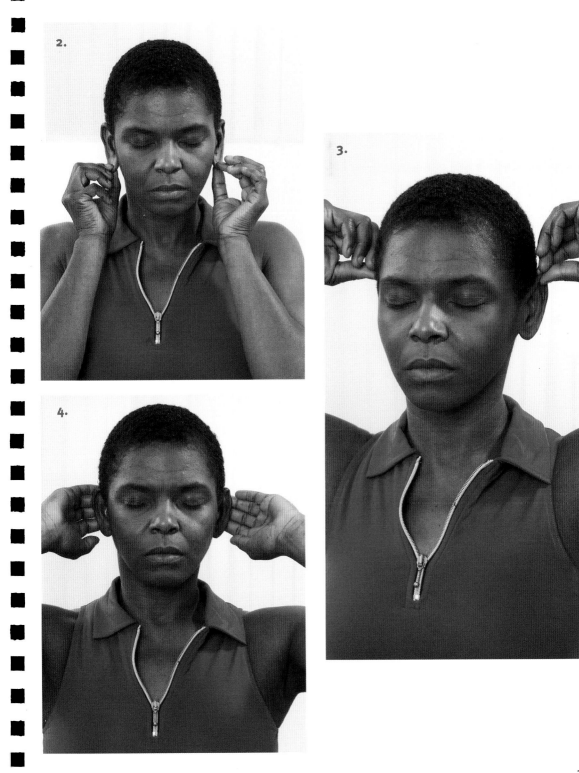

Reiki

Reiki (pronounced "RAY-kee") is a Japanese word meaning "universal life energy." It's similar to the "laying on of hands" practiced in some religions. The reiki master places his or her hands on various parts of a person's clothed body. The intention is to redirect spiritual energy within and around the person. It's believed that, when spiritual energy is channeled through the reiki master this way, the person's spirit can be healed. The spirit, in turn, can heal the person's body. A session usually takes about an hour. There's little scientific evidence to support the use of reiki. Nevertheless, some people say they find it quite relaxing and feel refreshed afterward.

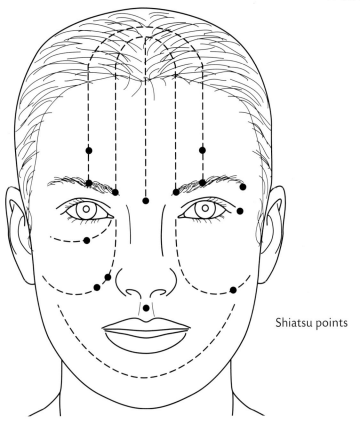

Shiatsu points

Shiatsu

Chinese culture doesn't have a monopoly on the concept of vital life energy. In ancient Greece, it was called *pneuma*; in India, it's called *prana*; and in Japan, it's called *ki*. Shiatsu is a Japanese finger pressure technique similar to acupressure that's intended to stimulate and balance the flow of this vital energy. Along with applying pressure to key points on the body, shiatsu practitioners also stroke and massage the areas corresponding to meridians. In addition, shiatsu treatments include gently rotating the limbs and stretching the muscles. The combination of hand pressure, massage, and stretching can be an effective way of releasing muscle tension and decreasing psychological stress.

While you can certainly learn about shiatsu and acupressure from books, locating precise points on the body takes some training and practice. It might be worth your while to sign up for a self-help workshop, if one is taught in your vicinity. In addition, a recent survey by the American Massage Therapy Association found that about 36% of its members offer shiatsu or acupressure. To find a qualified massage therapist in your area, check the association's website (www.amtamassage.org). For more information on choosing a massage therapist, see Chapter 8.

To find a provider who's also an acupuncturist, a good starting point in the United States is the National Certification Commission for Acupuncture and Oriental Medicine (www.nccaom.org). At this writing, 40 states also require that acupuncturists have state licensure or certification. However, the requirements vary from place to place, so don't be afraid to ask questions about training, experience, and credentials. Also, let the practitioner know if you have any health conditions that might affect the safety or effectiveness of a particular technique for you. The pressure or stretching shouldn't be painful, so speak up if it is. When it comes to shiatsu and acupressure, good communication is as vital as proper technique.

7: Yoga Methods

Tactic: Using yoga methods to calm your mind and relax your body.

For many people, the word "yoga" still conjures up the mental image of a lithe body in an impossible pretzel pose. However, yoga is actually a comprehensive system of mental and physical training that's practiced by millions of people—young and old, physically fit and out of shape, healthy and ailing. As a physical discipline, yoga uses special postures to stretch, strengthen, and align the body. As a mental discipline, it uses breathing exercises and meditation to calm the mind. The combination makes for a powerful mind/body approach to health and wellness that combats stress on multiple levels.

The Seven Chakras

The study of yoga dates back some 5,000 years to India. Its name comes from a Sanskrit word that can be variously translated as "union," "yoking," "effort," or "discipline." In other words, yoga represents an effort to unite the mind and body. Today, many people regard yoga strictly as a fun way to add variety to their exercise routine. Yet the breath work and meditation that lie at the heart of traditional yoga shouldn't be forgotten, if for no other reason than because they're great ways of reducing stress.

It's not necessary to understand or accept the philosophy underlying yoga to benefit from it. However, many people find that learning about yoga traditions can help them appreciate the ancient art and science behind the poses. Just as traditional Chinese medicine is based on qi, yoga is based on *prana*—the life-force energy that's believed to animate each person and the universe as a whole. A lack of *prana* leads to restlessness, apathy, and inertia, while the presence of this life force leads to energy, health, and vitality. The breath is thought to be the main source of *prana*, so breathing exercises are intended to improve the quality of *prana* within a person. Meditation helps regulate *prana* as well, while yoga

postures open up spaces inside the body that allow *prana* to circulate more freely, carrying life-giving energy with it.

According to yoga beliefs, the body contains seven main energy centers, called chakras (pronounced "CHAH-kruhs"). These chakras correspond roughly to segments of the spinal cord and brain. However, they are thought to be psycho-spiritual centers rather than strictly physiological ones. The lowest chakra, located at the base of the spine, is said to hold a powerful but often dormant form of energy, called *kundalini* energy. Certain meditation techniques are said to awaken this energy and allow it to rise up through the other chakras. When it reaches the highest chakra, located at the top of the skull, yoga philosophy holds that the result is enlightenment and awareness of your full potential.

To try a meditation based on the chakras, see the Chakra Check in Chapter 11.

Traditional yoga philosophy holds that each of the seven chakras within the body has a unique psycho-spiritual function:

Name	Physical Location	Psycho-Spiritual Function
Saturn	At the base of the spine	Source of *kundalini* energy, the dominant energy within a person. Connected to safety and survival.
Jupiter	In the lower abdomen	Source of creative energy. Connected to creativity and sexuality.
Mars	Behind the navel	Source of active energy. Connected to interpersonal trust and emotional authenticity.
Venus	Behind the heart	Source of compassionate energy. Connected to love and self-esteem.
Mercury	In the throat	Source of communicative energy. Connected to honest and direct communication.
Sun	On the forehead	Source of intuitive energy. Connected to personal vision and intellectual clarity.
Thousand Petalled Lotus	At the top of the head	Source of enlightenment energy. Connected to spirituality and self-realization.

Hatha yoga

While the philosophical roots of yoga may be interesting, it's the physical poses that are most familiar to people today. Hatha (pronounced "Haht-tuh") yoga is a general term for physical yoga. This type of yoga is usually taught in a group class, although many people practice it at home with the help of instructional books and videos. There are a number of different styles of yoga that vary in intensity and focus. Some are more relaxing and meditative, while others are more powerful and intense. Whatever the approach, however, most yoga classes provide a workout that improves flexibility, increases strength, and helps calm the mind while enhancing concentration.

Numerous studies have documented the physical and mental benefits of yoga. Many have shown that yoga can reduce stress, anxiety, and depression. Researchers have also found that yoga can be used to control physiological functions linked to the stress response, including blood pressure, heart rate, respiration, metabolism, and brain waves. In addition, there's evidence that yoga may help reduce symptoms and improve the quality of life for people with a wide range of medical disorders, including cancer, asthma, diabetes, arthritis, carpal tunnel syndrome, substance abuse, high blood pressure, heart disease, and migraines. As a result, more doctors are now recommending yoga as an adjunct to standard medical care.

All hatha yoga classes are centered around a carefully selected series of body postures, called *asanas*, and breathing techniques, called *pranayama*. The postures are performed while standing, sitting, or lying on a mat. They're done with focused concentration and careful attention to breathing and bodily sensations, making hatha yoga an ideal choice for moving meditation.

These are some of the most popular variants of yoga:

- **Sivanada—** This gentle, meditative form of yoga is a good option for beginners and those just looking for a relaxing experience. The poses are held for an unusually long period to allow ample time for the body to adapt and the mind to relax. Classes often begin and end with a short chant.

- **Iyengar—** This type of yoga focuses on body alignment and perfection of form. It often incorporates props, such as blocks, belts, benches, and cushions. Iyengar yoga is a good choice for beginners and those rehabilitating an injury, since it emphasizes proper technique at all times. However, it's also popular with athletes looking to improve their balance and flexibility.

- **Ashtanga—** Also known as power yoga, this style emphasizes muscular endurance as well as flexibility. Classes involve demanding moves, such as jumps, and continuous motion rather than static poses. Participants work up a sweat,

and even those in good shape may find ashtanga yoga a challenge. It's only appropriate for individuals who are seeking a strenuous workout.

- **Bikram—** Also known as hot yoga, this style is performed in a very warm room, typically kept at 80° to 105°F. Practitioners claim that the heat warms and stretches the muscles while flushing out toxins through sweat. However, exercising in such high heats can be dangerous for those who aren't accustomed to it or who have medical problems.

- **Kundalini—** This type of yoga emphasizes higher consciousness along with flexibility. It aims to awaken the energy within a person through intense breathing patterns, meditation, and sometimes chanting. Since the breath work is so demanding, it may not be appropriate for pregnant women and those with certain medical conditions, such as high blood pressure.

- **Viniyoga—** This style emphasizes the linking of poses in a conscious, methodical fashion. It also stresses focusing on the breath and adapting to the needs of an individual. The careful individualization of the movements is seen as more important than rigid adherence to a set form.

- **Ananda—** This type of yoga regards each posture as a means to the end of self-awareness. It also emphasizes relaxing deeply into the poses, based on the idea that they are actually a prelude to meditation.

If you decide to try yoga, your choice of style should be dictated by both your personal goals and your physical condition. If you have an injury, illness, or pain, ask your doctor if there are any moves you should avoid. Since your doctor probably won't be an expert on all the styles of yoga, it may help to take along a book with pictures illustrating the postures. Some restrictions may be necessary. For example, people with sciatica may need to avoid forward bends and intense hamstring stretches, while pregnant women and those with high blood pressure should

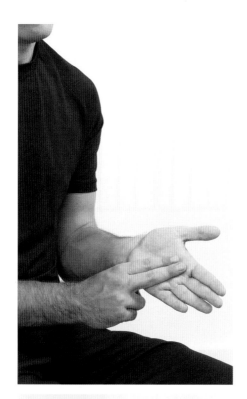

avoid holding their breath or doing upside-down poses, such as shoulder and head stands. Inform your yoga instructor of any physical limitations you may have. In addition, listen to your own body during practices, and don't do anything that feels forced or painful.

Yoga breathing

Focused breathing plays a role in many relaxation techniques. In yoga, however, breath control takes center stage. Tradition has it that vital life energy is found in the air we breathe, and yoga teaches how to make optimal use of this air for improved health and well-being. Most yoga breathing exercises use deep, abdominal breathing, in which the abdomen expands on each inhalation and constricts on each exhalation. The exercises also stress breathing through

the nose rather than the mouth. Nasal breathing slows down the process, since air must pass through two small holes instead of a single big one. It also gives the air a chance to be warmed, moisturized, and filtered inside the nose before it circulates through the rest of the body.

Yoga breathing can be used to call up the relaxation response, either alone or in tandem with meditation. These yoga-inspired exercises can be used for quick stress relief:

Side-to-side breathing

1. Sit in a comfortable position. Fold the pointer and middle fingers of your right hand into your palm. Inhale deeply (see the top left picture).

2. Press your thumb against the right side of your nose, closing off your right nostril. First exhale and then inhale slowly through your left nostril (see the bottom left picture).

3. Release your thumb, and press your ring and pinkie fingers against the left side of your nose, closing off your left nostril. First exhale and then inhale slowly through your right nostril (see the picture at bottom right).

4. Repeat Steps 2 through 3 several times as you focus on the breath going in and out.

Spine-tingling breathing

1. Sit in a comfortable position. Close your eyes, and bring your attention to the base of your spine.

2. Inhale slowly and deeply. As you do, draw your awareness up your spinal cord—up your back, then up your neck, and finally to your brain.

3. Exhale slowly. As you do, gradually bring your awareness back down your spinal cord to the base of your spine.

4. Repeat Steps 2 through 3 several times.

It's not uncommon to feel a little dizzy when you're first getting used to breath control exercises. If this happens to you, let your breathing return to normal and rest for a few minutes. Don't try to stand up until the dizziness has passed.

Mantra meditation

Meditation is another cornerstone of yoga practice. Just as there are many styles of hatha yoga, there are also several forms of yoga meditation. However, one of the most popular involves focusing intently on a mantra—a sound or word that has special meaning for the meditator. Traditionally, a mantra is thought to be imbued with spiritual power that can cleanse the mind and body of negative energy. For example, the classic mantra "om" is thought to be the sound of the universe vibrating. During meditation, it's said to clear the mind and instill a sense of oneness with all creation.

In modern times, the practice of focusing intently on a repeated sound, word, or phrase has been touted as a fast, easy way to call up the relaxation response. (For instructions, see the Relaxation Response in Chapter 11.) Interestingly, researchers have found that the technique works even better when people choose a personally meaningful focus word rather than a neutral word, such as "one."

Traditionally, mantras are thought to have sacred significance, and they're passed down from spiritual leaders to their students. However, if you're mainly interested in the relaxation benefit, you can certainly choose your own mantra. If you're religious, you might pick a word or phrase from your spiritual belief system, such as "Jesus is Lord," "hail, Mary," "Allah," or "shalom." If you prefer a nonreligious approach, you might select an inspirational phrase from a favorite song or book.

Just as yoga has special postures for exercise, it also has poses for meditation. Most involve sitting on the floor with the back straight but not rigid, and the legs crossed. A cushion can be placed under the seat for greater comfort. There are several advantages to the cross-legged position. For one thing, it creates a sturdy base for your body and tends to tilt your pelvis to just the right angle for supporting your spine. For another thing, keeping your seat on or near the floor is said to impart a sense of connection with the ground and, by extension, the world as a whole. In addition, many people find that they can maintain the easier cross-legged positions fairly comfortably for long periods. If you prefer to meditate in another position, however, there are several alternatives. These are some common poses used for meditation:

- **Easy seated pose** *(see below left picture)*— As the name implies, this is a very basic posture. It simply involves sitting cross-legged in a natural position, with the sides of both feet on the ground and the hands resting on the knees.

- **Lotus pose** *(see below, right picture)*— This is the classic posture that many people associate with meditation. In the easiest version, called a quarter lotus, one foot rests on the opposite calf rather than on the floor. The next step up is the half lotus, in which one foot rests on the opposite thigh (see opposite page, top picture). The most difficult version is the full lotus, in which both feet rest on the opposite thighs—a position few people can achieve and fewer still can maintain for any length of time.

- **Kneeling** *(see opposite page, bottom left picture)*— This position—called "Japanese-style" because it's favored in that country—is an alternative to sitting cross-legged. You sit back with your buttocks on your heels. For

greater comfort, you can place a cushion or a small, slanted bench between your buttocks and your feet. The Japanese name for this kind of specially-designed meditation bench is called a seiza bench.

• **Sitting in a chair** *(see below, right picture)*— Individuals who have trouble sitting down on the ground—or getting back up again— often find it easier to meditate while seated on a firm chair.

   If you try this, keep your legs uncrossed, your feet planted solidly on the ground, and your hands resting lightly on your thighs.

• **Corpse pose** *(see bottom picture)*— Although the name is unappealing, the pose is very comfortable. Just lie on your back with your arms extended about 6 to 8 inches away from your body and your palms up. Separate your legs by a foot or so. Although this is an effortless position, it can be a little too restful. You may find yourself drifting off to sleep.

From mantras to mudras

If you've ever wondered what to do with your hands during meditation, yoga has practical answers to this question as well. Over the centuries, a variety of hand postures, called mudras, have been devised. Traditionally, mudras are thought to redirect chakra energy, which is emitted from the fingertips. This task is accomplished by connecting the fingers and hands to each other in different ways.

• **Om** *(see opposite page, top left picture)*— This mudra is said to symbolize the union of divine energy with the self. The hand position is similar to an A-OK sign, with the tips of the thumbs and index fingers brought together to form circles and the rest of the fingers extended. Instead of raising the hands the way you would to signal A-OK, though, you lay them palms up on your knees while you're in a seated meditation posture.

• **Gnana** *(see opposite page, top right picture)*— This mudra symbolizes enlightened individuality. It's similar to the om mudra, except that the index finger touches the first joint of the thumb rather than the tip.

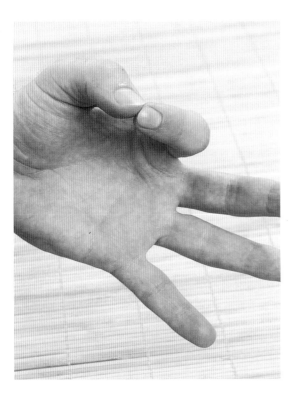

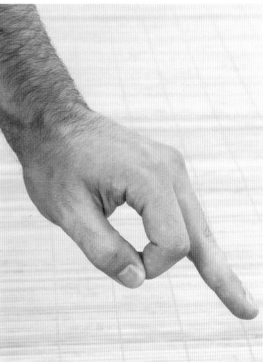

- **Prithvi** *(see right picture)*— This mudra symbolizes connection with the Earth. It's similar to the gnana mudra, but the palms are turned downward. You can rest your fingers on your knees.

- **Chalice** *(see page 86)*—This mudra symbolizes blissful energy. It's often used along with the lotus sitting positions. If your right foot is on top, cup the fingers of your right hand inside those of the left hand. If your left foot is on top, reverse the finger position. Then bring the tips of the thumbs together to form an oval space with your hands. Place your joined hands in your lap.

- **Gomukha** *(see page 87)*—This mudra symbolizes the union of mind and body. Interlace your fingers to form a cup. Your thumbs can lie on top of each other, or you can touch the tips. Place your joined hands in your lap.

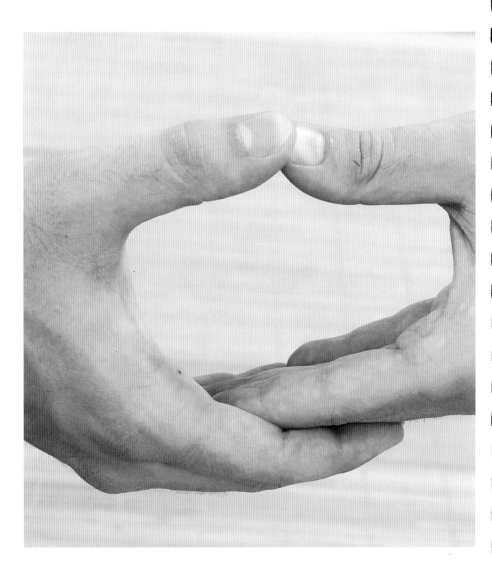

Yoga and you

Yoga means different things to different people. For some, it's just a pleasant way to relax and stretch. For others, it's a mental and spiritual way of life. Either way, you'll get more out of a yoga class if you take the time to look for one that's well matched to your needs.

If your goals are strictly stress- and fitness-related, you may find what you want at your neighborhood gym. On the other hand, if you're interested in exploring yoga philosophy in depth, your best bet may be a studio devoted exclusively to yoga.

There are no across-the-board certification standards for yoga teachers. However, several individual yoga schools do certify those who complete their training programs. In addition, some yoga teachers are also certified as personal

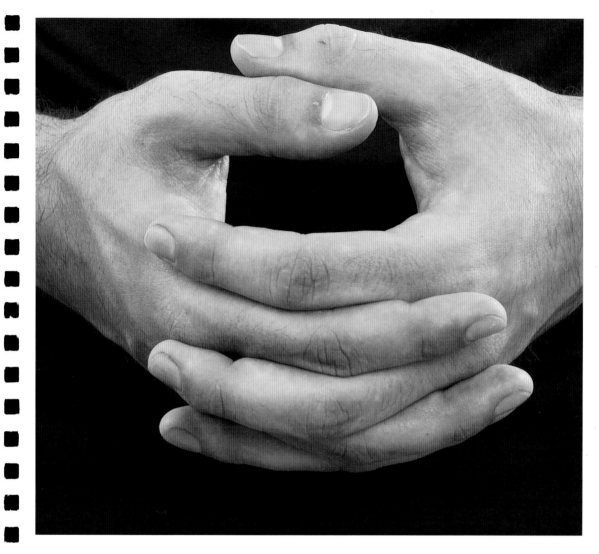

trainers or group-fitness instructors. Be sure to ask about training, certification, and orientation. In addition, ask whether you can observe a class or two before deciding to sign up.

Once you begin studying yoga, don't expect dramatic changes overnight. Like anything else, however, the more you practice, the sooner you'll see benefits. A regular class can help ensure that you're doing the poses properly. For the best results, though, you'll also need to practice at home between classes. Many people find that yoga first thing in the morning helps them get ready to face the day. Others find that a yoga session early in the evening helps them release pent-up stress. The marvelous thing about yoga is that it can be adapted to suit almost every schedule, lifestyle, and personality.

8: Exercise and Massage

Tactic: Relieving muscle tension through exercise and massage.

The stress response is designed to get your muscles ready to fight or flee. It's no surprise, then, that muscle tension is one of the cardinal signs of stress. If you can eliminate that muscle tension, you'll often find that the psychological stress vanishes with it. Stretching loosens up your muscles to relax your mind and help prevent aches, pains, and stiffness. It's an easy way to cut down on stress while you're sitting at a desk, standing in line, watching the kids, or doing almost anything. You might think that aerobic exercise, which makes the muscles tighten and work, would have the opposite effect. However, aerobic activities turn out to be great stress relievers, too, in part because they let you burn off muscle tension the way nature intended. Massage is yet another way to work out the kinks in tense muscles. There are many types of massage, but three of the most popular for stress control are Swedish massage, reflexology, and Indian head massage.

Stretching

Imagine yourself spending hours poring intently over financial records for your taxes. At first, you may be so preoccupied with figuring out how much you owe or searching for a crucial receipt that you don't realize how tense your muscles are getting. By the time you finish, though, you're sure to notice the ache in your upper back or the crick in your neck. Chances are, you'll be feeling pretty stressed out as well. Now replay the scenario in your mind, but this time imagine yourself taking brief stretching breaks as you work. Don't you feel better? Even if you never gave it much thought, you probably know intuitively that stretching is a great way to ward off tension-related discomfort and distress.

The nice thing about gentle, easy stretching is that it doesn't require any special skill, equipment, or clothing. With appropriate modifications, it can be done by just about anyone, anywhere. Since stretching is performed slowly and methodically, it's easily combined with slow, deep, even breathing. Using this combination, you can activate the relaxation response at the same time that you're releasing tension from your muscles, delivering a one-two punch to knock out stress.

Of course, stretching, like anything else, can be taken to an extreme. There's a big difference between the intense flexibility exercises practiced by ballerinas or yoga instructors, and the simple, gentle stretching you do first thing in the morning when you're just getting out of bed. What we're talking about here falls more into the latter category. While it may help you maintain your natural flexibility, gentle stretching won't drastically improve your range of motion. However, it can loosen up tight muscles and tendons so that you feel more comfortable and less stiff.

This kind of easy stretching is quite safe, but you should still use common sense and restraint. Don't push beyond your own limits. If a stretch hurts, you've gone too far, and you need to ease up immediately. Take your time. The secret to releasing tension from your muscles is to hold a mild stretch for 10 to 30 seconds. For best results, you should repeat each stretch a few times. If you're doing a stretch correctly, it should get easier as the seconds tick away and your muscles gradually loosen up. If it gets more uncomfortable the longer you stretch, you're straining too hard and missing the point.

Home stretch

One part of the body in which many people carry a lot of tension is the neck. Here are some easy stretches you can try the next time you're feeling up to your neck in hassles. By combining these stretches with deep breathing, you get two-for-one stress relief benefits:

1. Drop your chin toward your chest, and let the weight of your head stretch the back of your neck. Take three deep breaths, and feel your muscles relax a little more with each exhalation. Then return your head to the upright position.

2. Turn your head to the right, and look as far as you can over your right shoulder. Take three deep breaths, and feel the muscles on the left side of your neck relax a little more with each exhalation. Then return your head to the

center position. Do the same thing on the other side.

3. Repeat the entire sequence two times.

Another area that tends to get tied up in tension knots is the shoulders and upper back. When you feel as if you're carrying the weight of the world on your shoulders, try these simple stretches:

1. Interlace your fingers, and straighten your arms in front of you with the palms turned outward. Take three deep breaths, and feel the stretch in your shoulders, arms, and upper back.

2. Place your interlaced fingers behind your head, keeping your elbows extended to the sides. Gently pull the shoulder blades toward each other. Take three deep breaths, and feel the stretch in your shoulders, chest, and upper back.

3. Repeat the entire sequence two times.

To stretch your whole body, see the Gentle Stretches in Chapter 11.

Aerobic exercise

Aerobic exercise—aka endurance or cardiovascular exercise—refers to activities that increase your heart rate and breathing for an extended period of time. Examples include brisk walking, running, hiking, stair-climbing, bicycling, lap swimming, rowing, aerobic dancing, and sports such as soccer and basketball that include continuous running. Such activities use the large muscles in your arms and legs nonstop for several minutes.

If you think that a faster heart rate, rapid breathing, and increased muscular activity sound a lot like the stress response, you're right. Yet numerous studies have shown that aerobic exercise is a potent stress reliever.

What's the explanation for this apparent contradiction? For one thing, exercise gives you a healthy excuse to punch your arms, pump your legs, or otherwise burn off all that muscle tension. It also serves as a pleasant diversion. It's hard to think about stress when you're focused on pacing your run, winning a game, or simply enjoying the scenery while you walk. Also, even though the physical arousal you experience during a workout has some things in common with the fight-or-flight

needed to show whether the same holds true for humans running around a track. However, since scientists have recently found that human brains continue to make new cells even in adulthood, it seems plausible that regular exercise might help people pump up their brainpower and perhaps reverse one harmful effect of chronic stress.

The type of aerobic exercise that's right for you depends on your physical health and personal preferences. In general, though, organizations such as the American College of Sports Medicine and the U.S. Centers for Disease Control and Prevention recommend that most adults engage in moderate-intensity physical activities for at least 30 minutes on five or more days of the week. If you haven't exercised for a while, start out slowly, and build up your workouts gradually. If you have a medical condition that might limit your participation in certain activities, talk to your doctor about choosing a safe exercise program for you. With a few sensible precautions, the benefits of exercise are open to nearly everyone, including people of all ages, fitness levels, and physical abilities.

response, the all-important psychological perception is completely different. Running down a footpath in the park can be either fun or boring, depending on your attitude. However, running away from a mugger who jumps out of the bushes is just plain terrifying—and stressful.

In addition, exercise increases blood flow to the brain, releases hormones, and stimulates the nervous system. It can trigger the release of chemicals in the brain that produce a feeling of euphoria lasting for up to 2 hours afterward. The effect has been nicknamed the "runner's high," but it can follow any sort of vigorous workout. Besides instilling a sense of well-being, this natural high can alleviate anxiety and depression.

New research also suggests that exercise may have a positive effect on the hippocampus, an area of the brain that plays a key role in learning and memory. This is the same area in which long-term stress seems to cause the destruction of brain cells. In contrast, aerobic exercise seems to lead to the proliferation of brain cells in the region—at least in lab mice running on a wheel. More research is still

Exercising your rights

Reducing stress, anxiety, and depression would be reason enough to exercise. Yet research shows that aerobic exercise has a host of other positive effects as well:

- Lowering blood pressure and improving cholesterol levels

- Decreasing the risk of having a stroke or dying of a heart attack

- Reducing the risk of developing type 2 diabetes or colon cancer

- Building and maintaining strong muscles, bones, and joints

- Helping achieve and maintain a healthy weight

- Promoting feelings of self-esteem and optimism

Anaerobic exercise

Other forms of exercise can help reduce your pent-up tension as well. These stress-relieving, health-enhancing types of physical activity include:

- **Strength exercise**—Also known as resistance training or weight training. This refers to exercise that builds up muscles through the power of resistance, an opposing force against which the muscles must strain. The resistance can be supplied by dumbbells or barbells, weight machines, elasticized bands, or other devices. At one time, such exercises were mainly the domain of bulked-up bodybuilders. In recent years, however, researchers have found that people of both sexes, all ages, and every body type can benefit from regular strength training. This type of exercise strengthens muscles and bones, and it helps control blood sugar and cholesterol levels. It also boosts metabolism even while resting, which can help with weight control. In addition, strength training has been shown to increase self-confidence and decrease stress and depression.

- **Mind/body exercise**—Such activities emphasize mental focus as well as physical movement and proper breathing. T'ai chi and yoga are two examples that have been discussed already. Another popular option is Pilates, a method of body conditioning developed by Joseph Pilates in the early 1900s. Today, Pilates studios seem to be cropping up on every street corner. The exercises taught there improve flexibility and strengthen the core muscles of the abdomen and back, which support and stabilize the spine.
  Exercisers are encouraged to concentrate on the quality of execution rather than the quantity of repetitions. As with other types of mind/body exercise, Pilates can be used as a form of moving meditation.

Nutrition

When it comes to your overall health and well-being, exercise and diet go hand in hand. The foods you choose can fuel your stress or ease it by nourishing your brain and body. Unfortunately, "at the very time when people need to be eating their best, they tend to be eating their worst," says Elizabeth Somer, MA, RD, a registered dietitian who writes and speaks on the food-mood connection. Here are some general dos and don'ts:

• Do get adequate amounts of B vitamins. These vitamins help maintain the nervous system, which goes into overdrive during times of stress. A deficiency in B vitamins may make it harder to adapt to the increased demands, so it's important to get enough of these nutrients. Good food sources include chicken, legumes, fish, bananas, avocados, and dark green leafy vegetables.

• Do consider taking a multivitamin-mineral supplement. In addition to B vitamins, the demand for many other nutrients is increased during periods of stress. A moderate-dose multivitamin can provide extra nutritional insurance at such times. Of course, it's also essential to eat regular, balanced meals. Too many people react to stress by skipping meals or binging on junk food.

• Do drink plenty of fluids. The first sign of dehydration is fatigue, and fatigue is closely related to stress and depression. It's hard to feel relaxed and happy when you're exhausted. New guidelines from the Institute of Medicine recommend that men aim for about thirteen 8-ounce cups of water and other beverages daily. Women should aim for about nine cups.

• Don't overdo the caffeine. Coffee and other caffeinated beverages can have a dehydrating effect, since they cause increased urination. Three or more cups of coffee per day can also lead to the "caffeine jitters," which just magnifies anxiety. Coffee too close to bedtime can keep you awake at night. In addition, once a caffeine high wears off, heavy users may experience withdrawal symptoms, including depression and fatigue.

• Don't drink alcohol to excess. Many people overindulge when they're feeling stressed out. Unfortunately, the choices they make while under the influence are often anything but soothing. In addition, alcohol places added demands on the body, and it interferes with restful sleep.

• Don't rely on sugar for a quick pick-me-up. Many people crave sweets when they're under pressure. Eating a sugary snack can deliver a quick burst of energy, but it's soon followed by a crash. Before long, you may find yourself on an emotional rollercoaster of highs and lows. In the long run, this eating pattern actually creates more stress, leaving you feeling worse rather than better.

Swedish massage

Exercise is one way to use the body to calm a stressed-out mind. Massage is another. Essentially, massage refers to a wide variety of techniques that involve stroking, kneading, or otherwise manipulating the muscles and soft tissues. The soothing power of touch has long been recognized, and it comes as second nature to most of us. Think of the way a mother instinctively comforts her baby by patting and rubbing the infant's back. Massage has simply taken this natural instinct and codified it into a therapeutic system.

Almost every culture has a tradition of using the hands as healing tools. In Eastern Asia, these traditions include acupressure and shiatsu, discussed in Chapter 6. In the Western world, the most familiar method is Swedish massage, which uses long strokes, kneading, and friction on the top layers of the muscles. It's a full-body treatment in which oils or lotions are often used. Swedish massage can be gentle and soothing, or it can be vigorous and stimulating, depending on the speed and firmness of the strokes. This helps explain why it can have different effects on different individuals. Some feel drowsy after getting a Swedish massage, while others feel invigorated. In either case, however, the pleasure that a massage gives is usually enough in itself to make the recipient feel like a new person afterward.

Beyond that, massage can stretch tight muscles, releasing the tension there. Studies have found that it can also promote feelings of relaxation and wellness, and alleviate feelings of anxiety and depression. For certain people with chronic illnesses, research has shown that professional massage therapy can reduce pain, decrease joint stiffness, and rehabilitate injured muscles. Some research has also suggested that it may reduce blood pressure and promote better sleep.

The exact means by which massage exerts its positive effects is still unknown. However, there's evidence that it stimulates the nervous system, increases the flow of blood and oxygen to the cells, and enhances circulation in the lymph system—a network of organs, nodes, ducts, and vessels that is a major component of the body's immune response. Of course, the exact effects on a particular individual will depend on the technique used, the skill of the person giving the massage, and the mental and physical state of the person receiving it. For the best possible results, you may need to see a professional massage therapist. Nevertheless, even a basic massage that a partner gives you at home is a great way to untie the knots in tense muscles and promote relaxation.

The gentler Swedish massage techniques are generally safe and fine for most people to try on their own. If you're pregnant, ill, or injured, however, ask your doctor if there are any specific techniques you should avoid. Don't massage any part of your body that is painful or inflamed, or where the skin is broken. Let the person giving the massage know if something hurts or feels unpleasant. Also, keep in mind that different people have different comfort levels when it comes to being touched. Listen to your own feelings about what's right for you. If you feel more stressed rather than less so after a massage, try another approach next time.

For a full-body Swedish massage at home, you'll need a willing partner with whom to take turns. The nice thing about massage is that it's almost as pleasurable to give as to receive. After all, both parties get to enjoy the soothing benefits of touch. To set the stage for relaxation, pick a quiet spot. Dim the lights, and perhaps turn on some slow, soft music or put a few drops of aromatherapy oil in a diffuser. The room should be warm and free from drafts. Of course, a professional massage table is the ideal work surface, but a mat or quilt on the floor is a good substitute. A bed doesn't work as well, because the mattress absorbs too much of the pressure. If you'll be using oils or lotions, protect the surface with a towel. Have another towel or sheet handy for covering the part of your body that isn't currently being massaged. Even if modesty isn't an issue, you may still want to cover up to stay warm. If you have sensitive skin, choose any oils or lotions carefully, since some may cause an allergic reaction or skin breakout.

To heighten the relaxing effects of receiving a massage, try using the principles of mindfulness. Close your eyes, and focus all your attention on the sensations that you're feeling. If other thoughts come to mind, take note of them without attempting to analyze them. Then gently return your focus to the wonderful experience of hands-on relaxation.

Different strokes

You may need to experiment a little to find the type of stroke and amount of pressure that feels best to you. A gentle Swedish massage should be pleasurable, not painful. Don't hesitate to speak up if something is uncomfortable. When it's your turn to give the massage, be sensitive to your partner's needs. Remember that what feels fabulous to one person may be annoying or painful to another. These are some of the strokes that are commonly used in Swedish massage:

- **Effleurage** *(see opposite page, top left picture)*— A long, smooth, gliding stroke. It's often used to spread oil around, warm up the skin, and relax the muscles at the beginning of a massage. The hand glides gently across a body surface, such as the leg, arm, or back. Often, both hands are used together.

- **Petrissage** *(see opposite page, bottom left picture)*— A kneading stroke that may follow effleurage. Performed on fleshy parts of the body, it involves lifting up the skin along with the underlying muscle, then squeezing, rolling, and pressing the tissues like a baker kneading dough. The trick is not to pinch just the top layer of skin, but to reach down somewhat deeper into the tissues—not painfully deep, though.

- **Friction** *(see opposite page, bottom right picture)*— A stroke that warms up the muscles by rubbing tissue against tissue. Warm muscles are less tense and more pliable. In one common variation, the heel of the hand or fingertips are pressed firmly into the skin, then moved in a circular motion. To imagine what this feels like, think of the way the shampoo person might massage your scalp at a salon.

- **Vibration**— A stroke that literally shakes the tension out of muscles. In one version, the fingertips are pressed into the body, while the person giving the massage stiffens her arm and hand. The person then makes her entire arm shake as a unit, vibrating the tissues beneath her fingers. For relaxation purposes, the pressure should be kept fairly light.

- **Percussion**— A technique that involves tapping or striking the muscles in a steady rhythm. It can vary from light taps with the fingertips to karate-like chops with the sides of the hands or pounding with a loose fist. But the goal is always the same: to stimulate the muscles and skin while stopping short

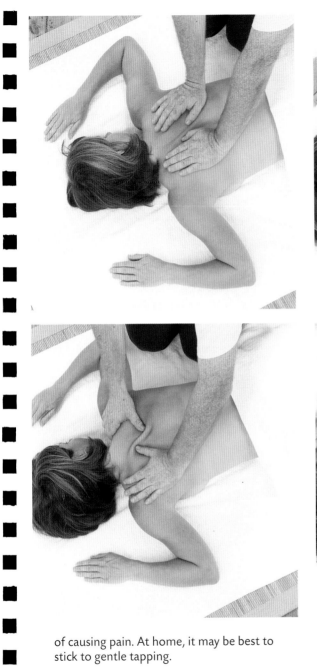

of causing pain. At home, it may be best to stick to gentle tapping.

- **Feather strokes** *(see top right picture)*— A form of effleurage that is often used at the end of a massage. The fingertips or hands are run very lightly across the skin in long, straight or wavy strokes. This stimulates the nerves. If

continued long enough, however, feathery strokes can be very calming.

For an example of a more limited massage you can give yourself, see the Hand Self-Massage in Chapter 11.

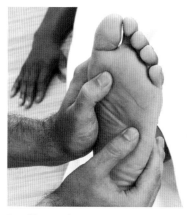

Reflexology

While Swedish massage can be used on the whole body from head to toe, reflexology focuses specifically on the feet and hands. It's based on the theory that there is a network of points in the feet and hands that correspond, or "reflex," to all the other parts of the body. By applying pressure to these points, practitioners claim that they can help treat a wide range of health problems.

This sounds similar to acupressure, and, in fact, reflexology may have been loosely based on ancient healing systems. However, its modern form was actually developed by an American doctor named William Fitzgerald, MD, in the late 1800s.

Fitzgerald proposed a system of healing that he called zone therapy. He believed that the human body could be divided into 10 vertical energy zones, each of which was controlled by certain areas on the extremities. Fitzgerald claimed that gentle pressure on these areas could relieve symptoms in the associated zones. Later followers refined his concepts and mapped out more specific points on the feet and hands.

Today, there are still many adherents who swear by reflexology. It's true that the extremities are rich in nerve endings, so it's possible that stimulating them could have effects on organs and tissues elsewhere in the body. Recently, several studies have reported positive results using reflexology to reduce the symptoms of conditions ranging from premenstrual syndrome and migraine to multiple sclerosis and cancer. Nevertheless, the medical theory behind reflexology remains controversial. It's still unclear how much of the benefit is due to reflexology itself and how much to the relaxing effects of getting what amounts to a foot or hand massage.

From the point of view of someone looking to relieve stress, however, the issue is probably moot. What really matters is that many people find reflexology very soothing. One advantage to this method is that you can do it on yourself, so you don't necessarily need to find a partner to help. Of course, if you do have someone who's willing to massage your feet or hands, it may be even more relaxing, since you can sit back and let the other person do the work. Another plus to reflexology is that it doesn't require you to disrobe or lie down, so it can be done just about anywhere.

As with other forms of massage, reflexology should not be painful if performed correctly. Don't try reflexology on a foot or hand if you have an injury, infection, or pain there. Also, avoid applying pressure to areas with varicose veins, and check with your doctor first if you have a chronic medical condition such as foot and toe problems, diabetes, arthritis, or carpal tunnel syndrome.

Otherwise, let your preferences and circumstances guide your choice of which extremity to work on. If you have a job that keeps you on your feet for hours, a foot massage may be just what you need at the end of a long day. On the other hand, if you spend your time typing at a computer, a hand massage may be wonderfully relaxing.

For an example of a routine that's intended mainly to feel relaxing rather than to stimulate specific target areas, see the Foot Self-Massage exercise in Chapter 11.

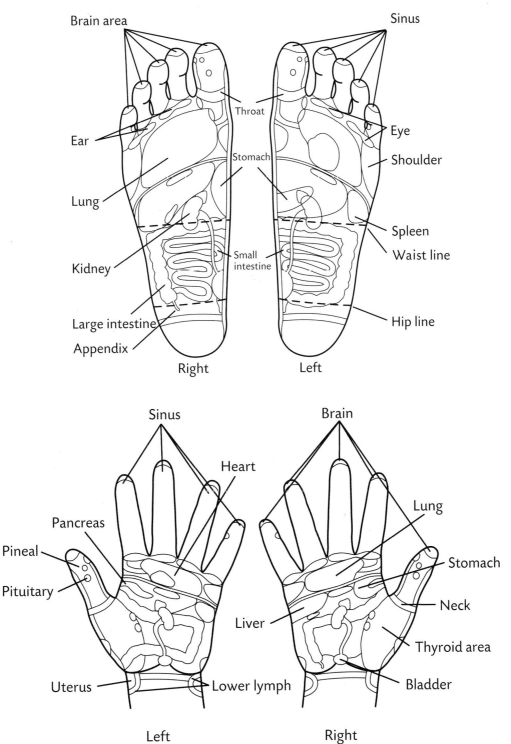

Brain area

Sinus

Throat

Ear

Eye

Shoulder

Stomach

Lung

Spleen

Waist line

Kidney

Small
intestine

Large intestine

Hip line

Appendix

Right

Left

Sinus

Brain

Heart

Pancreas

Lung

Pineal

Pituitary

Stomach

Neck

Liver

Thyroid area

Uterus

Lower lymph

Bladder

Left

Right

99

Indian head massage

Yet another form of massage that is rapidly gaining popularity as a stress reliever is Indian head massage. It's based on an ancient system of medicine called ayurveda, which has been widely practiced in India for over 5,000 years. A core concept of ayurveda is that illness occurs when a person's physical, emotional, and spiritual forces are out of balance with each other and the natural world. Stress is among the key factors that are thought to throw these forces out of whack. One of the main goals of ayurvedic therapy is to restore balance

and reinvigorate a person's body, mind, and spirit. Among the therapies used are diet, herbs, intestinal cleansing preparations, yoga, meditation, breathing exercises, imagery, and massage.

In India, massage is often a daily part of life. Indian head massage has evolved out of this tradition to become a fast-growing massage technique that is practiced worldwide. Although the name seems to imply that it's restricted to the head, this form of massage actually involves the neck, shoulders, and upper back as well. Since these are parts of the body that many people tense when under stress, getting a massage there can be especially relaxing.

Indian head massage is often done with the recipient seated and fully clothed, so it's convenient in many situations. It's also readily adaptable to self-massage. Whether you're giving the massage to yourself or having someone else do it, let your comfort guide how much pressure is applied to different areas. If you catch yourself tensing or flinching, that's a sign to lighten up. Don't try these techniques if you have an injury, infection, or pain in the region. Check with your doctor first if you have a chronic medical condition, such as osteoporosis or blood pressure problems, to make sure this type of massage is safe for you.

For an example of a relaxing routine you can try with a partner, see the Head and Neck Massage in Chapter 11.

Head lines

To see why head massage is so relaxing, try this simple experiment: Think of something annoying that has happened to you recently. Concentrate on how irritated you felt at the time. Then imagine yourself getting more and more upset, until you're really furious. Now notice how the muscles in your face feel. Is your forehead furrowed? Is your jaw clenched? It's little wonder that tension headaches and jaw pain are two very common symptoms of stress. By releasing all that tension from your face and scalp, you can often turn down the heat on your stress response, too. These two mini-massages can help.

Brow smoother

Place your index fingers side by side in the center of your forehead (see picture on right). As one moves up, the other moves down. Continue doing this as you walk your fingers apart to your hairline (see picture above). Then walk them back together again in the middle of your forehead. Repeat two times. This, and the following massages, can be done with a partner or on your own.

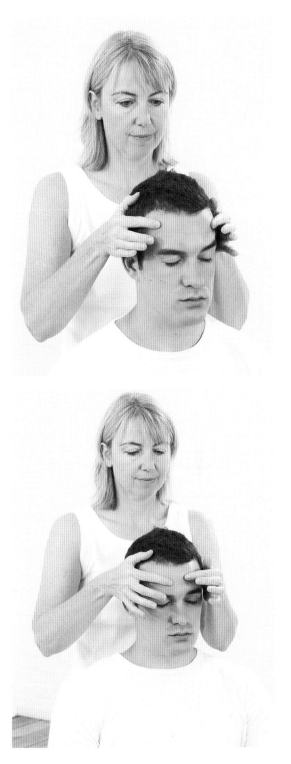

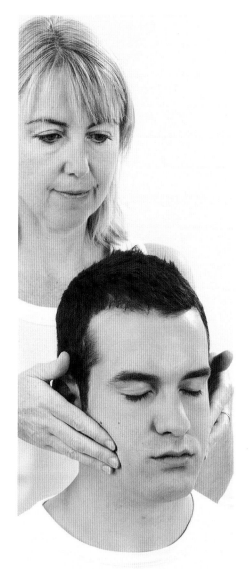

Jaw dropper

Place the four fingers of each hand next to each other on the chin (see above picture). Massage the muscles there in little circles. Then move the hands about half an inch apart, and massage some more (see left picture). Continue moving along the jawline this way until you reach the bottom of your ears. Then massage your way back to the chin again. Repeat two times.

Message on massage

There are many simple massage techniques you can try at home with a partner or even use on yourself. However, if you have special health concerns or if you just want to give yourself a treat, you may want to consult a professional massage therapist. Look for someone with appropriate training, experience, and credentials. In the United States, this means a massage therapist who is Nationally Certified in Therapeutic Massage and Bodywork (designated by the initials NCTMB). As of this writing, 33 states and the District of Columbia also require state licensure, certification, or registration. One place to start your search is the American Massage Therapy Association, which allows you to search for members on its website (www.amtamassage.org).

Expect to answer several questions about your overall health before the massage ever begins. "Tell the massage therapist if you have any pre-existing health conditions," says Judy Dean, MEd, NCTMB, chairman of the national certification board. "Also, let the massage therapist know if you're on any medication, especially a pain medication or blood-thinning drug."

Touch is a basic human need. Nevertheless, letting a stranger touch you, particularly if you're fully or partially unclothed, can make you feel vulnerable. Don't hesitate to speak up if anything makes you uncomfortable, either physically or emotionally. For a massage to be relaxing, it needs to feel safe and nonthreatening. The degree of trust and quality of rapport you have with the person giving your massage is often more important than the exact technique that's used.

9: Relaxing Pleasures

Tactic: Filling your mind with perceptions of pleasure rather than threat.

It's nearly impossible to feel threatened and delighted at the same time. That's the simple premise underlying some of the most potent stress-busters of all. These tactics fill your mind with pleasant sensations, feelings, and thoughts—and, in the process, crowd out more negative perceptions. The most direct route to the mind is through the senses, so it's not surprising that aromatherapy and music are two very effective ways to control stress. The sights, sounds, and smells of nature seem to have a particularly relaxing influence. In addition, a large body of research has found that social support from family and friends plays a crucial role in mental and physical health. For those so inclined, spirituality also seems to be a powerful antidote to stress.

Aromatherapy

The human body has several types of sensory receptors, but all have three things in common: First, they absorb physical energy from the environment. Second, that energy is converted into impulses within the body's nervous system. Third, the nervous system activity is organized into patterns that carry information about the world. Ultimately, the raw energy from the environment is transformed within the brain into perceptions of pleasure, pain, and everything in between. These perceptions, in turn, have a big influence on whether you feel happy and relaxed, or miserable and stressed out.

Aromatherapy uses fragrant substances distilled from plants to promote happiness, relaxation, and health. These substances, called essential oils, are highly concentrated extracts from grasses, leaves, flowers, needles, twigs, fruit peel, wood, and roots. The use of aromatic plants for healing purposes dates back at least to ancient Egypt, and many places around the world have a tradition of aromatherapy, including China, Tibet, India, the Middle East, Italy, France, and Australia. Today, aromatherapy is one of the fastest-growing areas of complementary medicine in the United States.

Essential oils can be diluted for use during massage. They can also be added to a bath or applied to the skin with a compress. In addition, they can be inhaled directly or added to a diffuser to disperse throughout a room. No matter which method is selected, however, research has shown that aromatherapy can have a measurable psychological and physiological impact. Of course, lovely smells may be enjoyed on a purely aesthetic basis. However, research suggests that aromatherapy may also be effective on a clinical level for reducing stress, anxiety, and depression as well as decreasing pain.

The power of smell is more understandable once you consider how the brain is organized. When odor molecules enter the nose, they're recognized by receptors found in hairlike fibers on nerve cells there. Signals from the nerve cells are then transmitted to the olfactory bulb, a small brain structure just above the nose. From there, messages are relayed to other parts of the brain—in particular, the forebrain, where they give rise to perceptions of smell, and the limbic system, where

they elicit emotional responses. The limbic system is especially important, because it's the seat of emotional memory. This helps explain why the scent of your father's pipe tobacco, your mother's homemade soup, or a lover's cologne can be so evocative years or even decades later.

Smell memory is the term used for a person's unique reaction to a particular odor based on learning. As you can imagine, a smell that is very soothing for one person may have precisely the opposite effect for another, depending on their past experiences. Nevertheless, certain aromas

What the nose knows

seem to have positive associations for most people, based on either learning or genetics. These associations, in turn, can be used to bring on feelings of calm and relaxation in the here and now.

Many kinds of aromas can arouse pleasant feelings. In fact, one handy stress-buster may be as close as your slow cooker. First thing in the morning, toss some veggies and other ingredients into the cooker to make a soup or stew. Then spend the rest of the day soaking up the aromas of home cooking. Of course, the big bonus is that you'll have a delicious, nutritious meal waiting at the end of the day.

Even very primitive organisms use chemical sense to move toward what's helpful (food) and away from what's harmful (predators). In fact, the limbic system of the brain actually evolved out of the olfactory system. For this reason, smell and emotion have a close evolutionary link. In fact, some researchers have gone so far as to argue that emotion is really just olfaction (the sense of smell) that has been intellectualized to a more abstract level. In any case, it's easy to see why odor can be such a powerful stimulator of stress, relaxation, and a host of related emotions.

Common scents

For the most reliable results, however, professional aromatherapists prefer the potency of essential oils. These aren't the same as the artificial perfumes and fragrances that are ubiquitous in products today. In fact, many aromatherapists caution against too much of a good thing. "I don't believe in blanket aromatherapy," says Jane Buckle, PhD, RN, a fellow in complementary and alternative medicine at the University of Pennsylvania. Instead, Buckle recommends a more judicious approach: the intentional use of powerful aromas at specific times, such as when you're in a particularly demanding situation or feeling the first signs of stress.

Rather than artificial fragrances, aromatherapists advise looking for natural, undiluted essential oils from reputable companies. The best suppliers usually include information on the label about the country of origin, the part of the plant used, and whether the oil is wild-crafted or organic. In addition, learn to compare apples to apples when buying essential oils, since oils with the same common name may actually come from different plants. Shop by botanical name (the Latin name, usually printed in italics) to make sure you're getting exactly what you want. Examples of essential oils that are reputed to promote relaxation include:

- Chamomile (*Chamaemelum nobile*)

- Clary sage (*Salvia sclarea*)

- Geranium (*Pelargonium graveolens*)

- Heliotropin

- Lavender (*Lavandula angustifolia*)

- Lemon (*Citrus limon*)

- Mandarin (*Citrus reticulata*)

- Roman chamomile (*Anthemus nobilis*)

- Sweet orange (*Citrus sinensis*)

- Ylang ylang (*Cananga odorata*)

Essential oils can be applied to the skin or dispersed into the air by a variety of means. Among the most common methods are:

- **Massage oil**— The essential oil is blended with a base material, such as sweet almond oil or apricot kernel oil. The National Association for Holistic Aromatherapy (www.naha.org) recommends a dilution of 10 to 20 drops of essential oil per ounce of base material.

- **Full bath**— The recommended amount is 5 to 10 drops of essential oil for a full-body bath. The water should be warm but not hot, and the oils should be added either after you're in the bath or right before you get in the water. Swirling around the water a little helps disperse the oil.

- **Foot or hand bath**— Add 5 to 7 drops of essential oil to a basin of warm water, and let the feet or hands soak for 10 to 15 minutes. This is said to be a particularly good way of battling stress and fatigue.

- **Compress**— Add 5 to 7 drops of essential oil to 2 or 3 cups of cold water. Swish the water around, then soak a washcloth in it. Wring out the cloth, and place it on areas where your muscles feel tense and stiff. Allow the compress to warm to your body temperature before removing.

- **Direct inhalation**— Put 2 to 4 drops of essential oil on a tissue. Hold the tissue close to your nose in the palms of your hands, and take several deep breaths through your nose. This works well as a quick stress reliever that can be used discreetly almost anywhere, including at work.

- **Steam inhalation**— Bring 2 cups of water to a boil. Carefully pour the water into a bowl, and add 2 to 5 drops of essential oil. Place your face about a foot away from the bowl, and close your eyes to avoid irritation. Then inhale the vapors for 5 to 10 minutes. You can drape a towel over your head to concentrate the vapors. If you notice any irritation, however, stop immediately.

• **Diffusers**— These are devices that disperse essential oils into the air. There are several kinds of diffusers on the market, including lamp rings, nebulizers, and clay pot, candle, fan, and electric heat diffusers. To compare the pros and cons of the various devices, one good starting place for information is the AromaWeb (www.aromaweb.com) website.

Never apply undiluted essential oil to the skin. When trying an essential oil for the first time, either on the skin or by inhalation, it's wise to start out with just a drop or two to check for irritation or an allergic reaction. Pay attention to all the safety information on the package as well. This is particularly important if you have a medical condition or are pregnant. Essential oils should not be taken internally, since many are poisonous. Also, be aware that essential oils are flammable, so keep them well away from fire hazards.

Music

Music is another timeless way to delight the senses while calming the mind. Ancient Greek philosophers believed that music could heal both body and soul, and Native Americans have long included singing as part of their healing rituals. In more recent decades, the healing power of music has been formalized in a science-based health profession known as music therapy.

within the ears. Thus, it may have a direct impact on physiology as well as psychology.

All you have to do is survey the selections in any music store to realize that musical taste is a very personal thing. The first rule of using music for relaxation is to pick something you genuinely enjoy. If a New Age-y mix of flutes and zithers sets your teeth on edge, forcing yourself to listen to it will only drive your stress level up. That being said, however, research has shown that certain kinds of music tend to be restful and relaxing for most people, most of the time.

Studies have found that tempos similar to the average human heart rate—about 40 to 60 beats per minutes—tend to be relaxing. Faster tempos, in contrast, tend to be stimulating, while slower ones may arouse feelings of suspense. In addition, soft, calm music is generally more relaxing than loud music that builds to a dramatic crescendo or inspires a strong emotional reaction. Repetitive and predictable rhythms are also more calming than unpredictable ones, and strictly instrumental selections may be less arousing than music with vocals. You want something that will put you in the mood to relax, not arouse you to think or feel strong emotions.

In addition, there's some evidence that high-pitched instruments may be especially soothing. "High pitches tend to be perceived as a little safer than low pitches," says Bill Thompson, PhD, a researcher who's a member of both the psychology department and the music faculty at the University of Toronto at Mississauga, Ontario. "It may be an evolutionary thing. In nature, high pitches are associated with smaller animals such as birds, while low pitches are associated with larger animals such as bears." Clearly, it makes good evolutionary sense for high pitches to signal safety and security, while low pitches set off mental alarms about a threat.

Music is easily combined with other stress control techniques—such as massage or stretching—to boost the benefits. With earphones, you can enjoy it in a wide variety of situations, from working at a desk to walking on a treadmill. For those who wish to take a more active approach, making music instead of just listening to it, music is also an ideal outlet for creativity and personal expression.

Studies have shown that listening to soothing music can decrease stress, anxiety, and depression as well as lower heart rate, blood pressure, and breathing rate. In medical settings, music therapy has been used to help people cope with everything from chemotherapy and surgery to insomnia and pain.

Researchers are still studying exactly how music has its salutary effects. However, one theory is that music distracts the mind, so that it can't focus on anxiety and worry. Another theory holds that the muscles, including the heart muscle, tend to synchronize with the beat of the music. Thus, slow music may slow down your heart rate, leading to a greater sense of relaxation. At the same time, your racing thoughts may decelerate as well to match the slower tempo. Still another theory suggests that, since sound is really vibration, it may resonate with every cell and tissue of the body, not only

Musical training

It's easy to put on your favorite song when you're feeling nervous or upset. However, it's also possible to use music to reset your mood in a more systematic way. Entrainment refers to a technique that first matches your current mood state, then moves you toward a more positive or pleasant frame of mind. To use the technique to turn a stressed-out mood into a relaxed one, make a recording that follows the pattern described below. Then play the recording anytime you need a little extra help calming down.

1. Pick a musical selection that fits your mood when anxious or agitated. For example, you might choose a piece of music that's fast-paced and low-pitched, with unpredictable rhythms and a jarring quality. Record a few minutes of this selection.

2. Pick additional musical selections that are gradually more and more soothing. Add a few minutes of each to your recording. The aim is to move systemically toward a piece of music that is relatively slow-paced and high-pitched, with predictable rhythms and a melodious quality. End with several minutes of this final selection.

3. Play the recording when you feel anxious or agitated, and try to match your mood to the music. By the time you get to the last piece, your breathing should be slow and even, and your mood should be in sync with the calm, restful quality of the music.

Nature

When it comes to counteracting the stresses and strains of modern life, the sights, sounds, and smells of nature seem to have a particularly profound impact. In one study from the Johns Hopkins University School of Medicine, researchers studied this effect in patients who were undergoing bronchoscopy, a diagnostic procedure in which a slender tube with a tiny camera attached is inserted through the nose or mouth into the lungs.

Patients who looked at a mural of a nature scene and listened to nature sounds through a set of headphones experienced less pain than those who didn't. This is probably a reflection of their lower level of stress. If it works for people having a tube pushed down their throats, then it can certainly work for you in more mundane situations.

One theory, called the biophilia hypothesis, suggests that the human brain is hardwired to respond positively to nature. You don't have to be a card-carrying tree-hugger to accept the logic of this premise. It only seems reasonable that humans might have an innate sensitivity to the flora and fauna with which we have coexisted in a close relationship since the dawn of humanity. Another theory holds that natural sights and sounds are simply pleasing diversions that distract people from thinking about more stressful things. Whatever the case, studies have shown that natural stimuli often work better than manmade ones for reducing stress.

The notion that communing with nature might be therapeutic is nothing new, of course. Through the centuries, natural settings have been associated with mental relaxation and restoration. During the Middle Ages in Europe, for example, hospitals were often located in monasteries, which also offered courtyards where patients could stroll or sit, and gardens where medicinal herbs were grown. In recent times, researchers have shown that looking at nature scenes is related to a decreased stress response, improved pain management, and faster healing.

The best way to avail yourself of this benefit is to get out into nature whenever you can. Even urban dwellers can enjoy regular strolls through the park, an afternoon at the botanical garden, or a weekend in the country. In addition, you can bring the great outdoors inside by taking these simple steps:

- Opening the curtains or blinds, if you have a view of natural surroundings

- Hanging a photographic mural of a restful nature scene on your wall

- Choosing a photographic nature scene for your computer screen saver

- Listening to a CD of peaceful nature sounds

- Adding an aquarium or potted plants to your home or office

- Decorating with natural objects, such as seashells, stones, or pinecones

- Buying a tabletop fountain, so you can listen to the soothing sounds of running water

Need a reminder to make time for simple pleasures? See the Random Bliss activity in Chapter 11.

Social support

Humans are by nature social beings. Now research has documented what most of us already knew: When you're stressed out and upset, it helps to turn to a friend or family member for support. The simple act of sharing your thoughts and feelings, and receiving caring and warmth in return, can go a long way toward reducing stress, anxiety, and depression.

Research has also shown that the more social contact people have, the less likely they are to develop physiological signs of chronic stress, such as high cholesterol and suppressed immune function. In addition, studies have found that a strong support network may help people ward off some illnesses, cope more effectively with the diseases they do have, and perhaps live a longer life.

On the flip side, social isolation seems to be one of the most stressful experiences there is. Think about the way isolation is used as the ultimate punishment for prisoners. A lack of supportive relationships can contribute to depression and undermine feelings of self-worth, purpose, and belonging. Of course, the wrong kinds of social contact can be equally stressful. It's difficult to feel relaxed when you're in the midst of a very abusive, oppressive, or rigidly demanding relationship.

Nevertheless, a relationship doesn't have to be perfectly conflict-free to be good for your mental health. It just needs to be based on genuine caring, mutual respect, and the implicit promise of emotional support—even if a few harsh words are exchanged now and then, or a few weeks occasionally pass without a phone call. To widen your social network, consider these simple strategies:

- Joining a local gym or signing up for an exercise class

- Taking a college course for fun or credit

- Getting involved in a hobby group devoted to one of your interests

- Volunteering for a cause you believe in

- Striking up a conversation with a neighbor or casual acquaintance

- Calling a friend you haven't seen lately

To nurture the bond with a loved one, see the Partner Meditation exercise in Chapter 11.

Pet therapy

There's nothing that says all of your friends have to walk on two legs. Animal companions offer unfailing loyalty and unconditional love. It comes as no surprise, then, that researchers have found that pet owners tend to experience less dramatic stress-related changes in blood pressure and heart rate than those without pets. In fact, pets may have an even more beneficial influence than human friends in some situations, perhaps because they aren't judgmental.

One study looked at stockbrokers who made more than $200,000 per year, lived alone, and had high blood pressure. All were put on blood pressure-lowering medication, and half were randomly chosen to get a dog or cat as well. Six months later, the stockbrokers were brought back in and asked to complete stressful tasks, such as pretending they were calming a furious client who had just lost $86,000 because of their bad advice. In the medication-only group, this task was enough to send their blood pressure shooting back up into the high zone. In the pet-owner group, however, blood pressure rose only half as much. According to the researchers, after the study was over and the stockbrokers learned about the results, many of those in the medication-only group bought pets of their own.

Spirituality

For many people, another major source of solace in stressful times is spirituality. Of course, there are innumerable ways of defining and expressing this spiritual leaning. In general, though, spirituality refers to a person's inward sense of connection to a higher power or meaning that transcends the individual. One outward manifestation of spirituality is religion, which may involve joining an organized group, participating in rituals, or adopting an established set of beliefs. As the term is used here, though, it's quite possible to be spiritual without being religious. All that's absolutely required is believing in something greater than oneself.

It seems as if a large majority of people are spiritually-oriented, based on this definition. In recent polls, about 95% of Americans say they believe in God or a higher power.

You don't necessarily have to understand something fully to benefit from it. Many people simply accept that spirituality is a wellspring of comfort and meaning in their lives. They don't need any outside evidence to validate their deep-seated convictions. For others, however, scientific evidence of the mental and physical benefits of spirituality only bolsters their beliefs. Recent studies have, indeed, lent strong support to the notion that spirituality is health enhancing.

Most controlled research has looked at religious behavior rather than spirituality per se, because it's easier to measure objectively. Studies have shown that people with strong religious faith are less prone to developing depression after stressful life events than their nonreligious peers. The deeper their faith, the less likely they are to be crippled by depression during and after hospitalization for a physical illness. Other research has found that people who regularly take part in religious services tend to have stronger immune systems and lower blood pressure than those who aren't regular participants. In addition, religious individuals tend to have fewer medical problems and live longer than their less religious counterparts.

There are several possible explanations for these findings. For one thing, spirituality and religion offer people a well-defined means of coping with stress, which may reduce their risk of stress-related illness. Spiritually-motivated people are also more likely to adopt healthy lifestyles, avoiding the harmful effects of smoking, substance abuse, and risky sexual behavior. In addition, being actively involved in a religious community may widen a person's social network. Finally, many people believe that optimal health depends on achieving the best possible balance of mind, body, and spirit.

Several classic stress management techniques—such as meditation, yoga, and reiki—can also be used as spiritual practices. If you belong to a religious group, you might want to get more involved by attending services more often, adding a study group, or volunteering for a community project. If one way you express your spirituality is through prayer, you might want to set aside a specific prayer time each day, so you make it a daily habit. These are some other ideas for nurturing your spiritual side:

- **Hold an inner dialogue.** Choose someone to act as your imaginary spiritual guide. This can be someone real or imaginary, alive or dead, famous or ordinary. Then imagine talking to that person, asking him or her for advice on how to handle a stressful situation in your life.

- **Find beauty in the mundane.** When you're feeling dispirited and drained, take a few moments to meditate intently on something beautiful in your surroundings. No matter where you are or what you're doing, there's bound to be something worth appreciating, whether it's the sight of sunlight dancing across the floor, the sound of children playing, the feel of air conditioning softly brushing your skin, or the smell of dinner cooking.

- **Cultivate your gratitude.** This approach was suggested by Krista Kurth, PhD, an executive coach who writes and consults about spiritual renewal in the workplace: Start a journal in which you record the things you're grateful for each day. Make a special effort to find things that inspire your gratitude even in tough situations or involving difficult people. Then, whenever you start feeling stressed, look back through the journal to remind yourself of all the positive things in your life.

Rather than viewing spirituality as the magical solution to all your problems, it may be more helpful to frame your spiritual quest as an ongoing search for personal growth. After all, if you start praying or meditating today, you may still wake up to conflicts and demands tomorrow. However, spirituality can provide a context for keeping those problems in perspective. Ultimately, this may reduce your stress while helping you find greater purpose and direction in your life.

10: Coping Strategies

Tactic: Using coping strategies that stop stress before it starts.

Many stress management techniques are geared to helping you control your response to stressful situations after they arise. However, the strategies in this chapter can stop many such situations from coming up in the first place. Time management tactics can help you better budget your time for improved efficiency and a healthier work/life balance. Communication skills can help you interact with others in a way that minimizes conflict and enhances

cooperation. When conflicts do arise, assertiveness skills can help you stand up for your point of view effectively without raising the stress quotient. Finally, goal-setting strategies can help you actually put all the stress control tactics in this book to good use. The ultimate goal: a happier, healthier, more relaxed you.

Time management

One of the most common sources of stress is having too much to do in too little time. While it might be nice to add a few more hours to the day, a realistic alternative is to make better use of the 24 hours you have. Time management strategies are intended to help you do just that. The first step is to identify the time-wasters in your daily schedule. This means tracking your daily activity patterns and looking for blocks of time that could be better spent. What it doesn't mean, however, is eliminating all the downtime you need for rest and relaxation. Half an hour used for sitting quietly and doing nothing but breathing may be time extremely well spent. On the other hand, half an hour used for pointless busywork is just 30 minutes you'll never see again.

For most people, routine chores eat up much of each day. Eliminate, delegate, or automate as many of these chores as you can. Try to streamline your procedures for handling the rest. For example, if email distracts you from getting other work done, you might set aside 20 minutes every morning for reading and answering email, and make a pact not to check your email box at other times.

Many people find that it helps to make a written schedule for each day's upcoming activities. Keep in mind, however, that life seldom goes exactly as scripted. Know which tasks really have to be done today and which can wait until tomorrow. Then tackle the essential tasks first, just in case you don't make it through the whole list. You can also plan for the unplanned by leaving a small block of time open for mini-crises and interruptions. By building flexibility into your schedule this way, you're less likely to feel stressed out by every slight deviation. Also, when you're filling up your calendar, don't forget to pencil in time for relaxation, socializing, and exercise.

If you're employed, it can be tricky to balance the competing demands of work and home. When you're at work, let family and friends know if there are times when you can't be disturbed except for true emergencies. When you're at home, resist the urge to take business calls or check work emails. Treat your time with the respect it deserves, and teach family, friends, bosses, and coworkers to do the same.

For more help identifying time-wasters, see the Day Planner in Chapter 11.

Clutter-busters

People vary widely in their tolerance for clutter. However, mess creates stress when it forces you to search repeatedly for mislaid items or makes you dread spending time in your own home or office. There's something to be said for the old adage "a place for everything, and everything in its place." Put the items you use most frequently in the most convenient locations, and stow away items you use infrequently. Then donate, recycle, or toss the rest. If the mess has really gotten out of hand, you might allocate 10 minutes each day for sorting through the clutter, starting with the worst area. You don't have to finish it all in a day or even in a week. Once things are organized, keep them that way by putting away items or discarding them as soon as you've finished using them. You may find that a more organized environment translates into a more orderly, less stressful life.

Communication

Another major source of stress for many people is interpersonal conflict. While occasional disagreements and annoyances are bound to arise in any relationship, constant fighting and backbiting can make life unpleasant for everyone. Good communication skills can go a long way toward averting many arguments and defusing volatile situations. When things get tense, use these strategies to keep them from escalating into a stressful scene:

- **Pick your battles.** Some conflicts really are just trivial irritations. If it won't matter to you tomorrow, it probably isn't worth hashing out today. Let it go.

- **Define the conflict.** Of course, some issues do need to be confronted. It helps to focus the conversation by stating up front what you believe the problem to be. If it's a multifaceted problem, don't tackle everything at once. Instead, concentrate on just one aspect, so that achieving a solution seems to be realistic.

- **Make "I" statements.** An accusatory tone will only put the other person on the defensive. Rather than discussing what you see as the person's bad behavior, it's usually more productive to talk about your own reactions, by using statements beginning "I think," "I feel," "I want," or "I need."

- **Stick to the facts.** Try to keep your emotions in check. Be alert for signs that your stress level is rising, such as angry or anxious feelings, unduly negative thoughts, faster breathing, a pounding heart, or a clenched jaw.

- **Take five to cool off.** If you start getting upset, try taking a few deep breaths and using cognitive reframing to calm down. If such strategies don't work, however, you may need a brief timeout. You can always buy a few minutes by excusing yourself to go to the bathroom or get a drink of water.

- **Be a good listener.** Try to listen to the other person's point of view with an open mind. Ask questions if you need any clarification. Occasionally repeat back your understanding of what the other person has just said, so you can check that the message you received is the one he or she intended to send.

- **Be ready to compromise.** Strive to find a solution that leaves each of you feeling as if you got at least part of what you want. First find the middle ground upon which you both agree. Then negotiate out from there.

- **Follow through, and follow up.** Once you've identified a mutually acceptable solution, do your part to implement it. Then check with the other person to make sure all is well from his or her perspective. The best way to minimize future conflict is by keeping the lines of communication open.

Assertiveness

Of course, it takes two people to find a compromise. If the other individual simply isn't willing to negotiate, a conflict may be unavoidable despite your best efforts. Such situations call for assertiveness—the ability to stick up for your rights and beliefs while still respecting those of the other person. It's quite different from aggressiveness, which means trampling on the rights of others, or passivity, which means ignoring your own wishes and needs. Instead, assertiveness is a more effective way of handling a conflict without fueling stress, anger, or frustration. These strategies can help you communicate your desires more assertively:

- **Define your request.** State what you want clearly and succinctly from the outset, limiting your request to one or two well-focused sentences. Don't expect the other person to read your mind. Spell it out!

- **Give your reasons.** Appeal to the other person's logical side by laying out the rationale for your position. Then describe your feelings to help the person also understand the emotional issues involved.

- **Connect your feelings to the other person's behavior.** Identify the problem behavior as specifically as possible. For example, instead of making the vague statement, "I feel hurt when you ignore me," you might say, "I feel hurt when you watch television while I'm talking to you."

- **Listen to the other person's side.** Give the person a chance to respond, and acknowledge the valid points he or she has made. For example, you might say, "I see what you mean. I did try to strike up a conversation while your favorite TV show was on. My timing could be better."

- **Look for a compromise.** Let the other person know that you have his or her interest at heart as well as your own. Try to find a win-win solution. For example, you might decide to reduce the amount of time spent watching TV, and to try not to interrupt each other during favorite shows.

To practice your communication and assertiveness skills, see the Role Playing activity in Chapter 11.

Goal setting

In the long run, goal setting is perhaps the ultimate stress control skill. Without the ability to set and attain appropriate goals, you're almost guaranteed to wind up feeling dissatisfied, frustrated, and stressed out. On the other hand, with this ability, you can successfully make positive changes in your life—including adopting a variety of other relaxation and stress control measures.

The first step to setting goals is to identify your core values. Companies phrase their values as a mission statement, and so can you. This should be a very general statement of your overall intentions and priorities. For example, you might decide that one of your overriding missions is "to stress less and relax more."

Once you've spelled out your mission, let it guide your future plans. Every time you formulate a long-term objective or short-term goal, check back to make sure it advances your mission. If it doesn't, it may not be aimed in quite the right direction. Try refining the goal until it seems to be aimed directly at the target value that you set.

The next step is to define your big-picture, long-term objectives. These are large goals you hope to achieve in a matter of months or years. Then pick one, and break it down into more manageable chunks that you might reasonably attain in days or weeks. To increase your odds of actually achieving one of these small, short-term goals, commit it to paper. Then tweak the wording until it's SMART:

- **Specific**—Goals should be narrowly focused. Ask yourself: Have you broken down a vague, sweeping objective into its specific, irreducible parts?

- **Measurable**—Goals should be quantifiable. Ask yourself: Can the outcome be stated as a number, percentage, or some other objective measure of success?

- **Action-oriented**—Goals should specify the action that needs to be taken to produce results. Ask yourself: Does the goal statement include an action verb?

- **Realistic**—Goals should be challenging but attainable. Ask yourself: Does the goal strike a happy balance between ridiculously easy and impossibly hard?

- **Time-limited**—Goals should have a deadline. Ask yourself: What is a realistic time frame for achieving this goal over the next several days or weeks?

For example, let's say your long-term objective is to begin meditating regularly. You might break that objective down into three progressively more difficult chunks: first, learning to use deep breathing to relax; second, focusing on deep breathing during short meditation sessions; and third, moving from focusing on deep breathing to focusing on other sensations during longer meditation sessions. Then you might turn the first chunk into a well-defined short-term goal: "to

practice deep breathing techniques every day, gradually building up to 20 minutes of deep breathing daily over a two-week period."

The final step is to develop an action plan that describes exactly what you'll do to attain your short-term goal. In the example, you might start by practicing deep breathing for 5 minutes at a time on a couple of days, then 10 minutes, then 15 minutes—until you finally build to the target of 20 minutes daily.

Problems and solutions table

If you...	Consider trying...	Found in Chapter...
Are bothered by disorder in your environment	Feng shui	6
	Clutter-busters	10
Are plagued by constant worrying	Therapeutic writing	5
	Thought stopping	5, 11
Are prone to frustration and self-doubt	Affirmations	5
	Cognitive reframing	5
	Goal setting	10
	Reframing journal	11
Are prone to pessimism	Affirmations	5
	Cognitive reframing	5
	Humor	5
	Reframing journal	11
Are troubled by time pressure	Time management	10
	Day planner	11

If you...	Consider trying...	Found in Chapter...
Don't have a massage partner	Ear points	6
	Head lines	8
	Foot self-massage	11
	Hand self-massage	11
Don't have time for a full body massage	Acupressure	6
	Indian head massage	8
	Reflexology	8
	Foot self-massage	11
	Hand self-massage	11
	Head and neck massage	11
Feel cooped-up indoors	Nature	9
	Walking meditation	11
Feel lonely and isolated	Pet therapy	9
	Social support	9
	Communication	10
	Head and neck massage	11
	Meditation on friendship	11
	Partner meditation	11

If you...	Consider trying...	Found in Chapter...
Feel out of touch with your body's signals	Breathing lessons	4
	Deep breathing	4
	Body scan	4, 11
	Progressive muscle relaxation	4, 11
Feel stressed-out by interpersonal conflict	Assertiveness	10
	Communication	10
	Role playing	11
Feel threatened by your environment	Imagery	5
	Safe haven	11
Have lost your sense of fun and playfulness	Humor	5
	Random bliss	11
Have trouble concentrating	Meditation	4
	Mindfulness meditation	4
	Quiet qigong	6

If you...	Consider trying...	Found in Chapter...
	Mantra meditation	7
	Mindful eating	11
Have trouble concentrating	Quiet qi meditation	11
	Sitting meditation	11
	Walking meditation	11
	Relaxation response	2, 11
Seek maximal results for minimal effort	Breathing lessons	4
	Deep breathing	4
	Progressive muscle relaxation	4, 11
	Shiatsu	6
	Home stretch	8
	Stretching	8
Seek to decrease muscle tension and stiffness	Swedish massage	8
	Indian head massage	8
	Gentle stretches	11
	Head and neck massage	11
	T'ai chi	6
Seek to increase physical fitness and health	Hatha yoga	7
	Aerobic exercise	8

If you...	Consider trying...	Found in Chapter...
Seek to increase physical fitness and health	Anaerobic exercise	8
	Nutrition	8
Seek to relax quickly and unobtrusively	Counting to 10	4
	Deep breathing	4
	Mini-meditations	4
	Cognitive reframing	5
	Ear points	6
Want to enhance sensory awareness	Body scan	4, 11
	Imagery	5
	Swedish massage	8
	Aromatherapy	9
	Music	9
	Music training	9
	Mindful eating	11

If you...	Consider trying...	Found in Chapter...
Want to learn more about traditional Indian methods	Chakras	7
	Hatha yoga	7
	Yoga breathing	7
	Indian head massage	8
	Chakra check	11
Want to learn more about traditional Eastern methods	Mindfulness meditation	4
	Acupressure	6
	Feng shui	6
	Qigong	6
	Reiki	6
	Shiatsu	6
	T'ai chi	6
	Quiet qi meditation	11
Want to promote spiritual awareness	Meditation	4
	Mindfulness meditation	4
	Reiki	6
	Chakras	7
	Spirituality	9

If you...	Consider trying...	Found in Chapter...
	T'ai Chi	6
	Hatha yoga	7
	Aerobic exercise	8
Have trouble sitting still	Anaerobic exercise	8
	Stretching	8
	Gentle stretches	11
	Walking Meditation	11

Goal tending

The better you get at setting and attaining goals, the more confidence you'll feel in your ability to handle challenges. On the other hand, if you're always aiming too high or planning too little, you're more likely to become plagued by self-doubt and a defeatist attitude. As a result, you'll feel more stress, since the stress response is based on your own perceived inability to cope with the challenges that come your way.

Thus far, we've been talking about formal, written goals. However, every conscious action you take is also based on informal, unspoken intentions. Such intentions need to be grounded in reality as well. If your intention in reading this book was to banish all stress from your life, you're doomed to end up disappointed and disillusioned. On the other hand, if your intention was to learn about ways to make stress work for you rather than against you, that's much more realistic. By practicing a variety of stress management techniques on a regular basis, you can learn to modulate your arousal, turning it down or up as the situation demands. Over time, you can draw upon these tactics again and again to refresh your mind, relax your body, and rejuvenate your spirit.

11: Stress Control Exercises

Relaxation response

To learn more:	Chapter 2
Time required:	10 to 30 minutes
What you'll need:	Nothing

1. Pick a focus word, phrase, or sound. Some people choose a word or phrase with personal meaning for them, such as peace, love, shalom, or hail Mary. Others prefer a sound, such as "om" (picture on right shows "om" in sanskrit).

2. Sit quietly in a comfortable position. Close your eyes, if you wish. You can also lie down, but this just makes it more likely that you'll drift off to sleep. Try to release all the tension from your muscles.

3. Breathe slowly and evenly. As you do, say your focus word, phrase, or sound on each exhalation. You can say it silently or aloud.

4. Passively disregard other thoughts that may arise. Don't worry about how well you're doing; you aren't competing in the relaxation Olympics. If distracting thoughts, feelings, or sensations come to mind, simply notice them without judging yourself. Then gently lead your wandering mind back to its focus point.

5. Practice once or twice daily. Start out for 10 minutes or less at a time. As the practice becomes easier, gradually work up to 20 minutes or more. Don't worry too much about meeting a time goal, however. It's more important to simply relax and accept the experience as it comes.

6. Don't end the session too abruptly. Take a few minutes to allow other thoughts to return gradually. Open your eyes and continue sitting quietly for a minute or two before standing. Give yourself a chance to savor the feeling of relaxation.

Sitting meditation

To learn more:	Chapter 4
Time required:	10 to 20 minutes
What you'll need:	Nothing

1. Sit quietly in a comfortable position. If you're seated in a chair, keep your legs uncrossed, your feet planted firmly on the ground, and your hands resting on your thighs. On the floor, many people find a cross-legged position easiest to hold for an extended period.

2. Close your eyes, if you wish, and try to release all the tension from your muscles.

3. Begin taking slow, deep, even breaths. Focus on the steady rise and fall of your breathing. Imagine the inhalations and exhalations as ocean waves, rolling up on the shore and rolling back out again in an eternal rhythm.

4. Passively disregard other thoughts that may arise. If distracting thoughts, feelings, or sensations come to mind, simply notice them without judging yourself. Some people find that it helps to name the thoughts; for example, by saying, "This is worry, this is worry, this is worry." By labeling the thoughts, you distance yourself from them, casting yourself in the role of outside observer. A little distance may make it easier to move on with your practice, gently guiding your focus back to your breath.

Walking meditation

To learn more: Chapter 4
Time required: 20 to 30 minutes
What you'll need: Nothing required, but some people prefer to use a treadmill or stationary bicycle

1. Find a safe place to walk that is well away from traffic, such as a treadmill or a footpath through a park. You can also adapt this activity to cycling on a stationary bicycle.

2. Start walking at your usual pace.

3. Breathe slowly and evenly as you walk. When you're ready, begin coordinating your steps with your breathing. For example, you might take four steps on each breath in and four more on each breath out.

4. Focus on the steady rhythm of your steps, passively disregarding other thoughts that may arise. If distracting thoughts, feelings, or sensations come to mind, simply notice them without judging yourself. Then gently lead your wandering mind back to the focus point.

5. Stay relaxed and comfortable as you walk. If you start to become winded, reduce the number of steps per breath.

Meditation on friendship

To learn more:	Chapter 4
Time required:	20 to 30 minutes
What you'll need:	Nothing

1. Sit quietly in a comfortable position. Close your eyes, if you wish, and try to release all the tension from your muscles.

2. Take several long, deep breaths to relax. Focus on the breath going in and out until your mind feels calm and receptive.

3. Think of something kind and generous that you have done for a friend. As you hold the image in your mind, remember the feeling of generosity that you had at the time. Take several minutes to focus on that feeling and contemplate its meaning. If distracting thoughts arise, gently return your mind to the focus point.

4. Let go of the image, and focus on the feeling alone. Notice how it feels to experience pure generosity.

5. Think of something kind and generous that a friend has done for you. As you hold the image in your mind, remember the feeling of gratitude that you had at the time. Take several minutes to focus on that feeling and contemplate its meaning. If distracting thoughts arise, gently return your mind to the focus point.

6. Let go of the image, and focus on the feeling alone. Notice how it feels to experience pure gratitude.

Mindful eating

To learn more: Chapter 4
Time required: 10 to 20 minutes
What you'll need: A piece of fruit

1. Sit quietly in a comfortable position with a piece of your favorite fresh fruit in front of you. Try to release all the tension from your muscles.

2. Take several long, deep breaths to relax. Let go of thoughts about the past and the future. Instead, bring your full attention to the present, focusing at first on your breath as it goes in and out.

3. When you're feeling relaxed, pick up the fruit. Focus intently on the experience of eating as if it were brand new to you. First, take a few minutes to notice the fruit's appearance, paying close attention to the shape, color, and texture.

4. Bring the fruit to your nose, and notice how it smells.

5. Turn the fruit in your hand, and notice how it feels. If it's a fruit that needs peeling, such as an orange or banana, take your time removing the peel. Notice how the peel separates from the fruit.

6. Begin to eat the fruit slowly and deliberately. Savor each bite as if you had never tasted the fruit before. If other thoughts come up, gently return your attention to the experience of eating. Let yourself fully appreciate the pleasures of looking, smelling, touching, and tasting.

Body scan

To learn more:	Chapter 4
Time required:	20 to 30 minutes
What you'll need:	Nothing required, but some people like to use a recording to guide them through the process

1. Lie down on your back in a comfortable place, such as on an exercise mat, on the floor, or in your bed. Close your eyes, if you wish. However, if you have trouble staying awake, it may help to keep your eyes open.

2. Take several long, deep breaths to relax. Let go of thoughts about the past and the future. Instead, bring your full attention to the present, focusing at first on your breath as it goes in and out.

3. When you're feeling relaxed, take a few moments to feel your body as a whole. Notice the sensations associated with the places where your body is in contact with the mat or bed.

4. Bring your attention to the toes of your left foot. Imagine directing your breath there, so that it feels as if you're first breathing in through your toes, then breathing out from them. It may help to think about your breath traveling down through your body—moving from your nose, into your lungs, through your abdomen and left leg, and into your toes. Then imagine the breath going back up again—moving through your body and out your nose.

5. Let yourself feel all the sensations from your toes. If you feel any discomfort there, don't fight it. Instead, accept it without resistance. Try to think about the discomfort objectively as if you were an outside observer. If you don't feel anything there at all, that's okay, too.

6. Move on to the next part of your body when you're ready. Try to leave any discomfort behind as you move from one part of the body to another. Gradually work your way through your left foot, left calf, left thigh, right toes, right foot, right calf, right thigh, abdomen, buttocks, chest, back, left hand, left lower arm, left upper arm, right hand, right lower arm, right upper arm, shoulders, neck, and face. Take your time as you really feel each body part and notice the sensations there without trying to change them.

Progressive muscle relaxation

To learn more:	Chapter 4
Time required:	20 to 30 minutes
What you'll need:	Nothing required, but some people like to use a recording to guide them through the process
Caution:	Check with your doctor first if you have an acute injury or a chronic pain condition. If tensing a muscle causes pain or cramping, stop immediately.

1.

1. Lie down on your back in a comfortable place, such as on an exercise mat on the floor or in your bed. Close your eyes, if you wish.

2. Take several long, deep breaths to relax. Focus on the breath going in and out until your mind feels calm and your body feels loose.

3. Bring your focus to your right hand and arm. Make a fist, and bend your elbow to about a 45° angle. Tighten your hand, forearm, and biceps. Hold for several seconds, and notice how the tension feels. Don't forget to keep breathing. Then release suddenly, letting your hand open and your arm fall back to the floor. Notice how the relaxation feels. Repeat the process.

4. Bring your focus to your left hand and arm. Perform Step 3 on the left side.

3.

4.

7.

5. Take a few more minutes to enjoy the heavy, relaxed feeling in both arms. Let them sink further into the floor.

6. Bring your focus to your face. Wrinkle your forehead, and squeeze your eyes closed. At the same time, bite down lightly, and pull back the corners of your mouth. Hold for several seconds, and notice how the tension feels. Then release suddenly, smoothing out your forehead and letting your jaw relax. Notice how the relaxation feels. Repeat.

7. Bring your focus to your neck. Bend your chin toward your chest without lifting the back of your head off the ground. Be careful not to strain your neck or tighten your muscles too hard. Hold for several seconds, and notice how the tension feels. Then release suddenly, letting your head roll back into its natural position. Notice how the relaxation feels. Repeat.

8. Take a few more minutes to enjoy the heavy, relaxed feeling in your head and neck. Let them sink further into the floor.

9. Bring your focus to your shoulders. Shrug your shoulders toward your ears. Hold for several seconds, and notice how the tension feels. Then release suddenly, letting your shoulders sink back into their natural position. Notice how the relaxation feels. Repeat.

10. Bring your focus to your chest. Expand your chest to make it wider. Hold for several seconds, and notice how the tension feels. Then release suddenly, letting your chest relax. Notice how the relaxation feels. Repeat.

11. Bring your focus to your abdomen. Squeeze your abdominal muscles tight. If you have trouble feeling this action, place a hand on your abdomen so that you can feel when your muscles get hard. Hold for several seconds, and notice how the tension feels. Then release suddenly, letting your abdomen relax. Notice how the relaxation feels. Repeat.

12. Bring your focus to your back. Arch slightly, being careful not to strain or tense the muscles too hard. Hold for several seconds, and notice how the tension feels. Then release suddenly, letting your back roll back into its natural position. Notice how the relaxation feels. Repeat.

13. Bring your focus to your buttocks. Tighten your muscles, feeling your pelvis tip up slightly. Hold for several seconds, and notice how the tension feels. Then release suddenly, letting your pelvis roll back into its natural position. Notice how the relaxation feels. Repeat.

14. Take a few more minutes to enjoy the heavy, relaxed feeling throughout your entire torso. Let it sink further into the floor.

12.

15. Bring your focus to your right leg and foot. Flex your ankle, pulling your toes toward you. At the same time, tighten the muscles of your calf and thigh, lifting your foot slightly off the floor. Hold for several seconds, and notice how the tension feels. Then release suddenly, letting your foot fall back into its natural position and your leg go limp. Notice how the relaxation feels. Repeat.

16. Bring your focus to your left leg and foot. Perform Step 15 on the left side.

15.

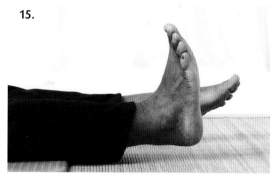

17. Take a few more minutes to enjoy the heavy, relaxed feeling in both legs. Let them sink further into the floor.

18. Continue lying quietly for several more minutes. Enjoy the feeling of heaviness throughout your whole body. Don't end the session too abruptly. Gently stretch and move different parts of your body for a few minutes before sitting up. You should feel pleasantly loose and relaxed.

18.

Reframing journal

To learn more: Chapter 5
Time required: 10 to 20 minutes
What you'll need: A notebook or computer

1. Set up a four-column chart in a notebook or on a computer. Label the columns Activator, Belief, Consequence, and Disputation.

2. Under the Activator heading, list a stressful event from the past 24 hours. The sooner after the event that you write about it, the fresher it will be in your mind, and the more helpful this activity is likely to be. If you don't have time to fill out the whole chart on the spot, try at least jotting down your immediate thoughts. You can flesh out the rest of the chart later.

3. Under the Belief heading, list the thoughts you had about the event at the time. Try to remember the first thoughts that came to mind.

4. Under the Consequence heading, list the emotions you felt and actions you took as a result of your beliefs and attitudes. Ask yourself: Did I feel distressed? Was I dissatisfied with the way things turned out?

5. Look back at your response under the Belief heading. Ask yourself: What objective evidence exists to support this idea? What evidence exists to refute it? Overall, does the belief seem to be false or distorted? If so, restate the thought in more accurate terms under the Disputation heading.

6. Imagine yourself replacing the original thought with the restatement from Step 5. Ask yourself: How might this have changed the consequences? Would I have felt less stress? Would I have handled the situation better?

Thought stopping

To learn more:	Chapter 5
Time required:	10 to 20 minutes
What you'll need:	A timer or a watch with an alarm

1. Write down several worrisome thoughts you have had in the past 24 hours. Don't evaluate the thoughts at this point. Just get them down onto paper.

2. After a few minutes, review your list. Go back through each item, and ask yourself: Is this thought unrealistically negative? Does it keep popping up uncontrollably at inappropriate times? Is the worry interfering with my ability to function effectively? Put a star next to any thoughts for which you answered yes to all three questions.

3. Pick a worrisome thought to use for this exercise, starting with the starred items. Set a timer or the alarm on your watch for 3 minutes. Then use the time to really focus on the selected thought, giving your worry free rein.

4. When the timer or alarm goes off, shout "Stop!" to interrupt the thought. You can also pinch yourself or pop yourself with a rubber band.

5. Let your mind go blank for a minute. If the worries return during this time, use the stop procedure again.

6. Repeat the whole process several times on different days until you can consistently stop worrisome thoughts this way. Then begin gradually weaning yourself off the stop procedure. For example, let's say you've learned how to halt worries by shouting "Stop!" The next step might be to say "Stop" aloud in a normal voice. Once you've mastered that, you can move on to giving yourself the command silently.

Safe haven

To learn more:	Chapter 5
Time required:	20 to 30 minutes
What you'll need:	Nothing

1. Sit quietly in a comfortable position. Close your eyes, if you wish, and try to release all the tension from your muscles.

2. Take several long, deep breaths to relax. Focus on the breath going in and out until your mind feels calm and receptive.

3. Imagine a place that makes you feel safe and cozy. This can be a real place, such as your favorite overstuffed chair or the kitchen from your childhood home, or a purely imaginary one. Whichever approach you take, however, try to make the scene seem as "real" as possible. Involve all of your senses in seeing, hearing, smelling, tasting, and feeling the experience.

4. Imagine yourself walking around and exploring your safe haven. Spend several minutes noticing every detail about this place.

5. Imagine yourself taking a seat or lying down in your safe haven. Spend several minutes enjoying the sense of safety and comfort.

6. Open your eyes, but don't rouse yourself immediately. Instead, take some time to enjoy the good feelings you generated. Try to transfer the safe feelings from your imagined place into your real-life environment.

Quiet qi meditation

To learn more:	Chapter 6
Time required:	About 10 to 20 minutes
What you'll need:	Nothing

1. Find a quiet spot where you can sit on the ground or a firm chair. Traditionally, a natural setting is thought to be best, but any place that is relatively free of distractions will do. Sit up comfortably straight, and rest your hands on your thighs, palms up.

2. Close your eyes, if you wish, and try to release all the tension from your muscles. Take several long, deep breaths to relax.

3. Focus on the sensations in the centers of your palms. Notice any changes in how your hands feel as you breathe in and out. Do you notice any warmth, heaviness, tingling, or pulsing there? If distracting thoughts arise, simply note them and gently guide your mind back to the focus point.

4. Gradually bring your focus to each thumb and finger tip in turn. Notice any changes in how they feel as you breathe in and out.

5. Bend your elbows to a 90-degree angle, so that your

1.

forearms rise off your thighs and extend in front of you. Keep your elbows loosely by your side, and turn your palms to face each other. Your fingers should be relaxed, but pointing straight ahead. Focus on the sensations in your palms. Notice any changes in how your hands feel as you breathe in and out.

6. Bring your focus to your breathing. As you breathe in, move your hands slightly farther apart. As you breathe out, move your hands slightly closer together. Notice any changes in how your hands feel as you continue this for several minutes.

7. Place your hands back on your thighs, palms up. Take a few more deep, relaxing breaths to finish.

5a.

5b.

Chakra check

To learn more:	Chapter 7
Time required:	20 to 30 minutes
What you'll need:	Nothing required, but some people like to use a recording to guide them through the process

1. Sit on the floor in a comfortable position. Many people find a cross-legged position easiest to hold for an extended period. If you're able, however, you can try one of the lotus poses described in Chapter 7.

2. Close your eyes, if you wish, and try to release all the tension from your muscles. Take several long, deep breaths to relax.

3. Bring your awareness to the base of your spine. Feel the connection between your spine and the ground below. Then imagine a little ball of red light there that slowly expands to fill your lower pelvic region with a warm, red glow. Repeat to yourself, "I am safe and secure." Spend a few minutes focusing on the repetition.

4. Bring your awareness to your lower abdomen. Imagine a little ball of orange light there that slowly expands to fill your lower abdominal region with a warm, orange glow. Repeat to yourself, "I am a creative being." Spend a few minutes focusing on the repetition.

5. Bring your awareness to the area behind your navel. Imagine a little ball of yellow light there that slowly expands to fill your upper abdomen with a warm, yellow glow. Repeat to yourself, "I can trust my feelings." Spend a few minutes focusing on the repetition.

6. Bring your awareness to the area behind your heart. Imagine a little ball of green light there that slowly expands to fill your chest with a warm, green glow. Repeat to yourself, "I am worthy of love." Spend a few minutes focusing on the repetition.

7. Bring your awareness to your throat. Imagine a little ball of blue light there that slowly expands to fill your neck with a warm, blue glow. Repeat to yourself, "I can tell the truth." Spend a few minutes focusing on the repetition.

8. Bring your awareness to your forehead. Imagine a little ball of indigo light there that slowly expands to fill your head from the eyebrows down with a warm, indigo glow. Repeat to yourself, "I can see things clearly." Spend a few minutes focusing on the repetition.

9. Bring your awareness to your forehead. Imagine a little ball of violet light there that slowly expands to fill your head from the eyebrows up with a warm, violet glow. Repeat to yourself, "I am transcendent." Spend a few minutes focusing on the repetition.

Gentle stretches

To learn more:	Chapter 8
Time required:	About 20 minutes
What you'll need:	A wall and a doorway
Caution:	Check with your doctor first if you have an acute injury, a chronic pain condition, or any medical condition that limits your mobility. If a movement causes pain, stop it immediately.

1. Stand perpendicular to a wall, about 2 feet away. Keeping your legs comfortably straight, lift your right leg a few inches off the ground in front of you. Put a hand on the wall for balance, if necessary. Slowly rotate your foot and ankle 10 times clockwise, then 10 times counterclockwise. You should feel your ankle loosen up. Repeat on the other side.

2. Turn to face the wall. Place both hands on the wall at shoulder height, standing back far enough to straighten your arms. Bend your left leg, and step your right foot back a few feet. Keeping your right leg straight, press your heel and foot flat into the floor. You should feel a gentle stretch in your right calf. If you don't, step your foot back a little farther. Hold for 20 seconds. Release. Repeat on the other side. Do the whole thing two more times.

3. Continue facing the wall, adjusting the distance as needed. Bend forward from your hips (not your waist) to place both hands on the wall at shoulder height, keeping your back straight. Slide your hands down the wall just far enough to feel a gentle stretch in the backs of your thighs. Depending on your flexibility, you may end up with your back parallel to the floor. Don't hunch up your shoulders. Hold for 20 seconds. Release. Repeat two more times.

4.

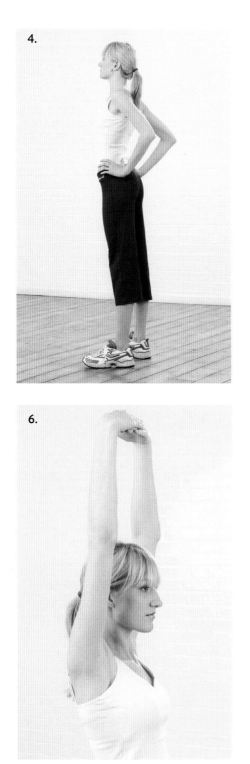

6.

4. Stand comfortably with your feet shoulder-width apart. Place your palms on your lower back with your fingers pointing downward. Gently push forward with your hands to create a slight arch in your lower back. Don't push beyond your comfort zone. Hold for 20 seconds. Release. Repeat two more times.

5. Move into an open doorway. Place your hands on either side of the doorway at shoulder height. Lean forward until you feel a gentle stretch in your chest. Keep your chest lifted. Hold for 20 seconds. Release. Repeat two more times.

6. Stand comfortably in the middle of the room. Stretch your arms straight up with your fingers interlaced and palms turned upward. Imagine your palms pressed against the ceiling. You should feel a gentle stretch in your shoulders, arms, and upper body. Hold for 20 seconds. Release. Repeat two more times.

7. Bend your right arm behind your head, with your elbow pointing upward. Grasp your right elbow with your left hand, and pull it gently toward the left until you feel a stretch in the back of your right upper arm. Hold for 20 seconds. Release. Repeat on the other side. Do the whole thing two more times.

8. Press your palms together in front of your chest in a praying position. Then, keeping your hands pressed together, raise your elbows until your lower arms are as nearly parallel to the floor as possible. You should feel a gentle stretch in your wrist. Hold for 20 seconds. Release. Repeat two more times.

9. Lower your right ear as close as you can to your right shoulder without raising the shoulder. You should feel a gentle stretch in the left side of your neck. Keep your shoulders relaxed. Hold for 10 seconds. Slowly lift your head back into its normal position. Repeat on the other side. Do the whole thing two more times.

10. Take a few deep breaths, and enjoy the feeling of relaxation and looseness throughout your whole body.

8.

9.

9.

147

Hand self-massage

To learn more:	Chapter 8
Time required:	About 20 minutes
What you'll need:	Nothing
Caution:	Don't massage an injured, infected, or painful hand, or press on an area with varicose veins. Check with your doctor first if you have a chronic medical condition that might affect your hands, such as arthritis, diabetes, or carpal tunnel syndrome. If massaging a spot causes pain, let up immediately.

1. Grasp your left thumb, and pull slowly and gently outward. Take three long, deep breaths. Repeat on each of the fingers of your left hand.

2. Press your right thumb into the palm of your left hand. Rotate the thumb in little circles on that spot. Continue for several seconds. Then move to another spot and repeat. Keep this up until you've covered the whole palm.

3. Place your left hand on your lap or a table, palm down. Press your right forefinger against the outside base of your left thumb. As you take a long, deep breath in, slowly trace up the outside of the thumb to the thumb tip.

4. As you let the breath out, slowly trace down the inside of the thumb to the inside base. As you take a deep breath in, slowly trace up the side of the index finger to the

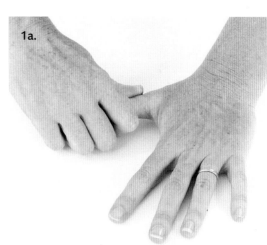

1a.

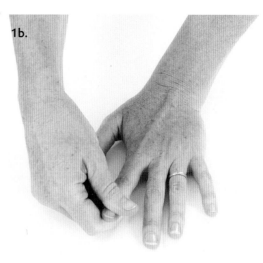

1b.

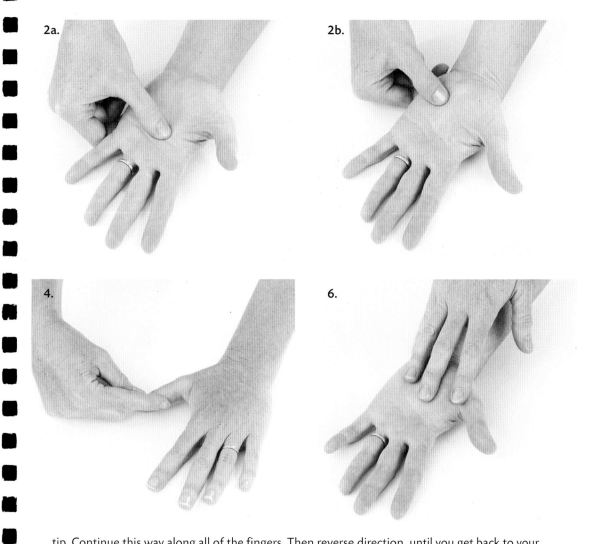

2a.

2b.

4.

6.

tip. Continue this way along all of the fingers. Then reverse direction, until you get back to your starting point.

5. Turn your left hand over, palm up. Loosely interlace the tips of your right fingers with those on your left hand.

6. Slowly drag your right fingertips down your left fingers, palm, and wrist in a very light, feathery motion. Repeat for a minute or two. At first, this may tickle a bit, but soon it should feel very soothing.

7. Repeat all of the above steps on the other hand.

Foot self-massage

To learn more:	Chapter 8
Time required:	About 20 minutes
What you'll need:	Nothing
Caution:	Don't massage an injured, infected, or painful foot, or press on an area with varicose veins. Check with your doctor first if you have a chronic medical condition that might affect your feet, such as foot and toe problems, diabetes, or arthritis. If massaging a spot causes pain, stop immediately.

1. Sit on a chair. Plant one foot on the ground, and lift the other one, crossing it comfortably over the opposite thigh.

2. Grasp the inside of your foot. Place both hands side by side just below the toes. The thumbs should be on the sole of the foot, and the fingers should be on the top of the foot. With the hand closer to the toes, gently turn the foot away from you. Keep the hand closer to the ankle stationary. Then, with the hand near the toes, gently turn the foot toward you, still keeping the hand near the ankle static. Repeat this back-and-forth motion several times.

3. Reposition both hands slightly closer to the ankle. Repeat Step 1. Continue moving your hands down the foot this way until the hands are just above the ankle.

4. Grasp the ball of your foot with both hands. One hand should be holding the inside of the foot, and the other hand, the outside. Place the thumbs on the sole of the foot a little below the big toe and second toe. Place the fingertips on the corresponding area on the top of the foot. Gently push the foot down and away from you with the right hand, and up and toward you with the left hand. Reverse. Try a figure of eight motion. Repeat this several times.

2.

5. Reposition your hands on the second and third toes. Repeat Step 3. Do the same on the third and fourth toes, and the fourth and fifth toes.

6. Cup the back of your heel loosely with the hand on the same side of the body, placing your thumb below the ankle bone. With your other hand, grasp the ball of the foot just below the toes. Using the hand by the toes, slowly and gently rotate the foot in a clockwise direction several times. Repeat in a counterclockwise direction.

7. Grasp the ball of your foot with the hand on the same side of the body, placing your fingers on top and your thumb on the sole. With your other hand, grasp the big toe. Slowly and gently rotate the toe in a clockwise direction several times. Repeat in a counterclockwise direction.

8. Apply Step 7 to each of the toes in turn.

9. Repeat all of the above steps on the other foot.

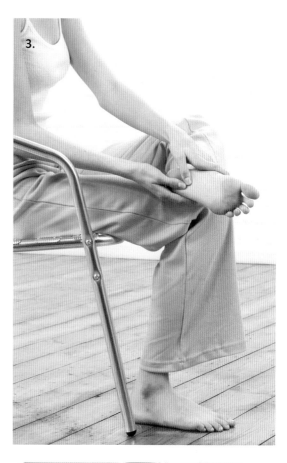

3.

4.

6.

Head and neck massage

To learn more:	Chapter 8
Time required:	About 20 minutes
What you'll need:	A partner and a firm chair
Caution:	Don't massage the head or neck if the person receiving the massage has an injury, infection, or pain in the area. Check with a doctor first if the person has a chronic medical condition, such as osteoporosis or blood pressure problems, that might make head or neck massage risky. If a massage stroke causes pain, stop it immediately.

1. Give the massage to a partner first. This both familiarizes you with the technique and demonstrates it to your partner. Later, you can take your turn as the recipient. Have the other person sit in a firm chair. If the person has long hair, clip it up while you work on her neck. Ask the person to sit up comfortably straight. Stand directly behind them and rest your hands gently on their head. Take a few minutes to allow your breathing to synchronize with the other person's.

2. Place one hand on the person's forehead. Have them tilt their head forward slightly, resting the weight of their head in your hand. With the fingertips of your other hand, make a series of firm, smooth, gliding strokes down the sides and back of their neck to warm and relax the tissues there.

3. Release the person's head. Place both of your hands on their shoulders with your thumbs on either side of the spine at the base of the neck. Apply steady pressure with the thumbs while rotating them in little circles at that spot. Let the person's comfort level guide how firmly you press. Then move

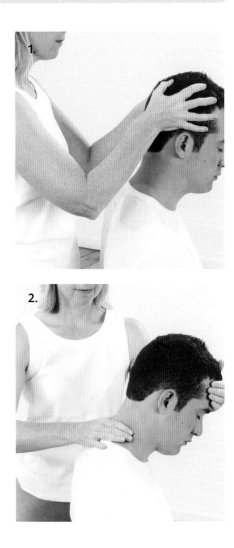

your thumbs up about half an inch. Press the thumbs into the muscles on the sides of the spine, and rotate. Keep working your way up the neck until you reach the base of the skull. Repeat the whole process two times, each time slightly farther from the spine.

3.

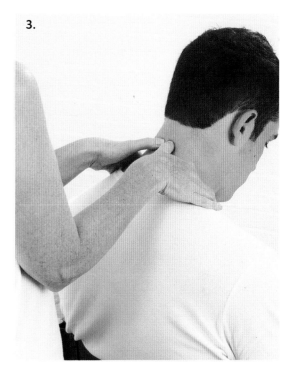

4. Stroke your fingertips down the sides and back of the person's neck again, much like in Step 1. This time, however, keep your strokes very light and feathery. Continue for a couple of minutes. If they start to get goosebumps, then keep up the light strokes until the goosebumps subside.

5. Unclip the person's hair, if it's up. Place both hands on top of their head and take a few moments to allow your breathing to synchronize again. Then, pressing with the palms of your hands, make circular

4.

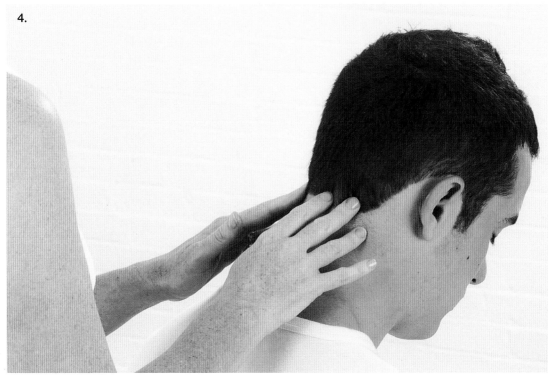

movements. You should feel the scalp moving over the skull. Reposition your hands and repeat. Keep this up until you've covered the entire scalp, but check to make sure this is comfortable.

6. Place your fingertips on the person's front hairline. Rotate your fingertips in little circles, as if you were shampooing the person's hair. Reposition your hands slightly, and repeat. Keep this up until you've covered the entire scalp.

7. Hold both hands above the scalp. Use your fingertips to gently tap all over the scalp in a steady rhythm. Keep your wrists loose, and let your fingers rebound off the scalp, like raindrops bouncing off the sidewalk.

8. Comb lightly through the person's hair with your fingers, separating the hair but not touching the scalp. Continue for a couple of minutes.

6.

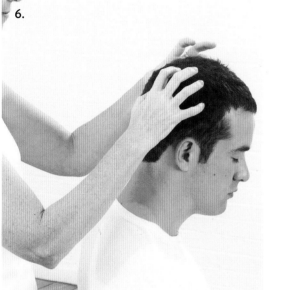

7.

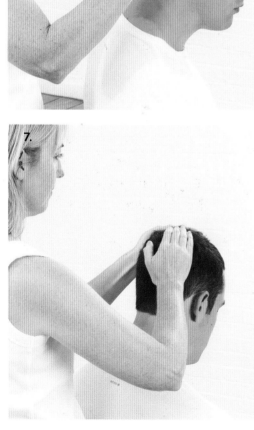

8.

Random bliss

To learn more: Chapter 9
Time required: 10 to 30 minutes
What you'll need: An empty jar and slips of paper

1. On several slips of paper, list easy ways of relaxing that work well for you. If you want, you can color-code the slips. For example, blue might stand for things you can do by yourself, and green might stand for things you can do with other people. Or, you could use white for activities that take 20 minutes or less, and yellow for ones that take longer than 20 minutes. Any system that suits your needs is fine. Keep the activities simple; for example, meditating, reading a favorite book, stretching, going for a walk, getting or giving a massage, listening to soothing music, or having a long, hot bath.

2. Mix the slips together in a jar. When you're feeling stressed, pick a slip at random, and spend 10 to 30 minutes enjoying that activity.

3. Keep adding to your jar as you expand your repertoire of stress control methods.

Partner meditation

To learn more: Chapter 4
Time required: 10 to 20 minutes
What you'll need: A partner

1. Sit quietly on the floor facing your partner. Try both sitting cross-legged, touching at the knees and holding the other person's hands. If this position isn't comfortable, try standing face to face about arms' length apart, with both hands placed on the other person's shoulders.

2. Begin taking slow, deep, even breaths. At first, both partners should focus on the rhythmic rise and fall of their own breathing.

3. Bring your focus to the other person, trying to match your breathing to your partner's. As your partner inhales deeply, you exhale fully. As your partner exhales fully, you inhale deeply. Continue for a few minutes as you and your partner both try to relax into the rhythm of the other person's body.

4. When one of you is ready, squeeze your partner's hands or shoulders to signal that it's time to move on to the next stage. While you both close your eyes, each should try to visualize the other as fully relaxed. In your mind's eye, watch your partner's face soften, body relax, and tension seep away. Imagine the deep calm and relaxation that your partner is feeling.

5. When one of you is ready, squeeze your partner's hands or shoulders to signal that it's time to move on to the next stage. While you both slowly reopen your eyes, try to match your breathing once again. Continue for a few minutes as you and your partner savor the sense of connectedness.

Day planner

To learn more: Chapter 10
Time required: 20 to 30 minutes spread throughout the day
What you'll need: A notebook or computer
Note: This activity is geared to managing your time at work, but it can easily be adapted to time management at home as well.

1. Think about the activities that make up a typical workday for you. Lump your daily work tasks into three or four primary categories. For example, you might decide that your activities consist of Routine Tasks, Current Projects, Planning and Development, and Relaxation and Socializing.

2. Determine the ideal proportion of time that you would like to allocate for each category. For example, you might decide that you want to spend 15% of your work time on Routine Tasks, 25% on Current Projects, 50% on Planning and Development, and 10% on Relaxation and Socializing.

3. Set up a four-column chart in a notebook or on the computer. Label the columns Time, Activity, Minutes, and Category. Under Time, divide the workday into 30-minute increments. Under Activity, you'll briefly note your main activities during each 30-minute block of time. Under Minutes, you'll list how much time you spend on each activity, and under Category, you'll note which of your categories each activity falls under. (See the sample daily work log on the following page.)

4. Record how you spend each 30-minute block of work time. Jot down your activities as close to the end of every half-hour as possible. That way, your memory will be fresh, so your record will be more accurate. (Don't stress out if you miss a few blocks of time, though.) Be completely honest, too. If you spend 10 minutes staring off into space, put that in your log.

5. At day's end, tally up how much total time you spent on each category of tasks. If possible, repeat the process for two or three days in a row, so that patterns become more obvious. Then compare the actual proportion of time you spent on each category to the ideal proportion you established earlier. Look for opportunities to use your time more efficiently. For example, if you're wasting too much time on routine tasks, you might look for ways to eliminate, automate, or delegate some of those activities. If you're not making enough time for relaxation, you might remind yourself to take stretch breaks a few times a day.

Date:	November 21		
Categories:	1 = Routine tasks, 2 = Current projects, 3 = Planning and development, 4 = Relaxation and socializing		
Time	Activity	Minutes	Category
8:00–8:30	Signing correspondence	10	1
	Answering emails	15	1
	Practicing presentation	5	2
8:30–9:00	Practicing presentation	25	2
	Stretching at desk	5	4
9:00–9:30	Working on marketing plan	30	3
9:30–10:00	Talking with coworkers	5	4
	Updating paperwork	15	1
	Talking to client on phone	10	2
10:00–10:30	Talking to client on phone	5	2
	Finishing up marketing plan	25	3

Role Playing

To learn more:	Chapter 10
Time required:	10 to 20 minutes
What you'll need:	A partner

1. Think of an interpersonal situation that's causing you stress, and have your partner do the same. Don't choose situations that involve each other. For example, if your partner is your spouse, you might focus on a conflict with a coworker. The person with whom you're having problems is called the Stressor.

2. Make a list of 10 things the Stressor might say that would make you feel anxious or angry. Have your partner make a list for his Stressor, too.

3. Take turns role playing the stressful scenarios. For the first 3 to 5 minutes, have your partner play the role of your Stressor, including as many statements from your list as possible. During this time, try using your deep breathing and cognitive reframing skills to remain calm and look at the situation objectively. In addition, try using your communication and assertiveness skills to calm down the stressor and lead the conversation down a more constructive path.

4. Spend a few minutes afterward discussing what just happened. What things did you try that worked well? What things could you have improved? Later, you can put these insights to good use in the real situation.

5. Repeat, this time taking the role of your partner's Stressor. As before, discuss the results afterward, and try to offer helpful feedback.

6. Take a few more minutes to just relax and unwind together. Remember that you're not each other's Stressors in real life, so don't let any negative feelings aroused by the role playing carry over into the rest of your day.

Resources

Stress, relaxation, and mind/body health

Books

Benson, Herbert, and Eileen M. Stuart. *The Wellness Book: The Comprehensive Guide to Maintaining Health and Treating Stress-Related Illness*. New York: Fireside; 1992.

Benson, Herbert, with William Proctor. *The Breakout Principle: How to Activate the Natural Trigger That Maximizes Creativity, Athletic Performance, Productivity, and Personal Well-Being*. New York: Scribner; 2003.

Davis, Martha, Elizabeth Robbins Eshelman, and Matthew McKay. *The Relaxation and Stress Reduction Workbook* (5th ed.). Oakland, CA: New Harbinger; 2000.

Elkin, Allen. *Stress Management for Dummies*. New York: Wiley; 1999.

Freeman, Lynn. *Mosby's Complementary and Alternative Medicine: A Research-Based Approach* (2nd ed.). St. Louis, MO: Mosby; 2004.

Goleman, Daniel, and Joel Gurin. *Mind/Body Medicine: How to Use Your Mind for Better Health*. Yonkers, NY: Consumer Reports Books; 1993.

Mason, L. John. *Guide to Stress Reduction* (rev. ed.). Berkeley, CA: Celestial Arts; 2001.

Sapolsky, Robert M. *Why Zebras Don't Get Ulcers: A Guide to Stress, Stress-Related Diseases, and Coping*. New York: W.H. Freeman; 1994.

Smith, Linda Wasmer. *Of Mind and Body*. New York: Henry Holt; 1997.

Tivieri, Larry Jr., and the American Holistic Medical Association. *The American Holistic Medical Association's Guide to Holistic Health: Healing Therapies for Optimal Wellness*. New York: John Wiley and Sons; 2001.

Wilson, Paul. *Instant Calm*. New York: Plume; 1995.

Winner, Jay. *Stress Management Made Simple: Effective Ways to Beat Stress for Better Health*. Santa Barbara, CA: Blue Fountain; 2003.

Websites

American Psychological Association: Stress
www.apa.org/topics/topic_stress.html

Mind/Body Medical Institute
www.mbmi.org

National Center for Complementary and Alternative Medicine
www.nccam.nih.gov

University of Pittsburgh Medical Center: Healthy Lifestyle Program
healthylifestyle.upmc.com

Breathing and meditation

Bodian, Stephan. *Meditation for Dummies*. New York: Hungry Minds; 1999.

Farhi, Donna. *The Breathing Book: Good Health and Vitality Through Essential Breath Work*. New York: Henry Holt, 1996.

Kabat-Zinn, Jon. *Full Catastrophe Living: Using the Wisdom of Your Body and Mind to Face Stress, Pain, and Illness*. New York: Delta; 1990.

Nichol, David, and Bill Birchard. *The One-Minute Meditator: Relieving Stress and Finding Meaning in Everyday Life*. Cambridge, MA: Perseus; 2001.

Mental approaches

Burns, David D. *Feeling Good: The New Mood Therapy* (rev. ed.). New York: Avon; 1999.

Lusk, Julie T. *30 Scripts for Relaxation, Imagery, and Inner Healing*. Duluth, MN: Whole Person Associates;1992.

Rossman, Martin L. *Guided Imagery for Self-Healing: An Essential Resource for Anyone Seeking Wellness* (2nd ed.). Tiburon, CA: H.J. Kramer; 2000.

Seligman, Martin E.P. *Learned Optimism: How to Change Your Mind and Your Life*. New York: Pocket Books; 1990.

Eastern methods

Chuen, Lam Kam. *Step-by-Step Tai Chi: The Natural Way to Strength and Health*. New York: Fireside; 1994.

Lundberg, Paul. *The Book of Shiatsu: A Complete Guide to Using Hand Pressure and Gentle Manipulation to Improve Your Health, Vitality, and Stamina*. New York: Fireside; 2003.

Sollars, David W. *The Complete Idiot's Guide to Acupuncture and Acupressure*. Indianapolis, IN: Alpha Books; 2000.

Yu, Tricia. *Tai Chi Mind and Body*. New York: DK Publishing; 2003.

Yoga methods

Carrico, Mara, and the Editors of Yoga Journal. *Yoga Journal's Yoga Basics: The Essential Beginner's Guide to Yoga for a Lifetime of Health and Fitness*. New York: Henry Holt; 1997.

Finger, Alan, with Al Bingham. *Yoga Zone Introduction to Yoga: A Beginner's Guide to Health, Fitness, and Relaxation*. New York: Owl Books; 2000.

Lusk, Julie T. *Desktop Yoga: The Anytime, Anywhere Relaxation Program for Office Slaves, Internet Addicts, and Stressed-Out Students*. New York: Perigree; 1998.

Payne, Larry, and Richard Usatine. *Yoga Rx: A Step-by-Step Program to Promote Health, Wellness, and Healing for Common Ailments*. New York: Broadway Books; 2002.

Exercise and massage

Anderson, Bob. *Stretching at Your Computer or Desk*. Bolinas, CA: Shelter Publications; 1997.

Bentley, Eilean. *Head, Neck, and Shoulders Massage: A Step-by-Step Guide*. New York: St. Martin's Griffin; 2000.

Brown, Denise Whichello. *Teach Yourself Indian Head Massage*. Chicago: Contemporary Books; 2003.

Budilovsky, Joan, and Eve Adamson. *The Complete Idiot's Guide to Massage*. Indianapolis, IN: Alpha Books; 1998.

Herdman, Alan, with Jo Godfrey Wood. *Coffee Break Pilates*. Gloucester, MA: Fair Winds Press; 2003.

Kunz, Barbara, and Kevin Kunz. *Reflexology: Health at Your Fingertips*. New York: DK Publishing; 2003.

Relaxing pleasures

Buckle, Jane. *Clinical Aromatherapy: Essential Oils in Practice* (2nd ed.). Philadelphia: Churchill Livingstone; 2003.

Keville, Kathi. *Aromatherapy for Dummies*. New York: Wiley Publishing; 1999.

Koenig, Harold G. *The Healing Power of Faith: How Belief and Prayer Can Help You Triumph Over Disease*. New York: Touchstone Book; 1999.

Ornstein, Robert, and David Sobel. *Healthy Pleasures*. Reading, MA: Addison-Wesley; 1989.

Coping strategies

Epstein, Robert. *The Big Book of Stress Relief Games: Quick, Fun Activities for Feeling Better*. New York: McGraw-Hill; 2000.

Gordon, Douglas. *Self-Management and Goal Setting*. Cincinnati, OH: South-Western Educational Publishing; 2000.

Morgenstern, Julie. *Time Management From the Inside Out*. New York: Owl Books; 2000.

Rouillard, Larrie A. *Goals and Goal Setting: Achieving Measured Objectives* (rev. ed.). Menlo Park, CA: Crisp Publications; 1998.

Author Bio

Linda Wasmer Andrews, MS, (www.LindaAndrews.com) has been coping with the deadline pressures of freelance journalism for more than two decades, so she knows a thing or two about stress. She specializes in writing about health, psychology, and the mind/body connection. Linda is the author of six previous books, including a Scientific American book titled *Of Mind and Body* and a children's book titled *Meditation*. She has also contributed articles to national magazines, major websites, and numerous reference works. Linda became so fascinated by the mind/body health topics she covered as a journalist that she recently returned to school to earn a master's degree in health psychology. She works from her home in Albuquerque, New Mexico, where she likes to breathe deeply, think optimistically, stretch regularly, and spend time doing nothing at all with her husband and two dogs.

Acknowledgments

All photographs © Chrysalis Image Library / Eddie MacDonald apart from the following.

B = Bottom L = Left T= Top

© Corbis / SIE Productions 110.

© Chrysalis Image Library 19, 37B, 58, 74, 104, 106, 108, 114, 121, 129. / Mike Prior 69, 77, 78.

© Digital Vision 6, 8L, 12, 13B, 13T, 14, 18, 25, 28, 29T, 29B, 31B, 35T, 37T, 40, 44T, 44B, 47, 50, 52, 55, 57T, 57B, 61, 62, 63, 64, 65, 67, 70, 90, 91, 105, 111, 112, 113, 116.

© Getty Images / Royalty Free 15, 32, 34, 35B, 46, 51, 118.

© Rex Features / John Powell 16.

© Stockbyte 33, 39B, 47B, 53, 92, 93, 94, 100.

All Illustrations © Chrysalis Image Library / Kuo Kang Chen apart from page 66 © Chrysalis Image Library / Robyn Neild.

Index